The Philosophy of The Plan of Salvation

The Philosophy of The Plan of Salvation

by James B. Walker

Bethany Fellowship INC.
MINNEAPOLIS, MINNESOTA 55438

Originally published in 1887 by
Cranston & Stowe

The Philosophy of the Plan of Salvation
James B. Wallker, D.D.

Library of Congress Catalog Card Number 80-69727
ISBN 0-87123-469-6

Published by Bethany Fellowship, Inc.
6820 Auto Club Road
Minneapolis, Minnesota 55438

Printed in the United States of America

INTRODUCTION
TO THE CHAUTAUQUA EDITION.
By H. B. Ridgaway, D. D.

WHILE religion and human nature remain essentially the same, it must needs be that the proofs which meet the objections to religion will remain essentially the same. The current objection to Christianity in Bishop Butler's day was based upon a Deistic view of the world; hence he aims to show that the same difficulties meet us in both natural and revealed religion, and that the objections which would be fatal to revealed religion would be alike fatal to all religion.

The miraculous element in the Gospels has uniformly been the stone of stumbling to skeptics. Yet from substantially the following position it is impossible for believers in supernatural Christianity to recede: "We must posit a nature to be acted upon, so fixed in its course that when any departure therefrom takes place we can be quite sure that it is not a mere random variety in the order of phenomena, but the result and proof of the action upon nature of higher spiritual powers. On the other hand, while positing a nature thus fixed in its course we must bear in mind that this course was meant to be acted on by a class of powers altogether different from physical forces. These forces are wills."

Huxley allows the argument of Hume against miracles from *experience* to be weak and unsatisfactory, and yet he himself virtually admits that hardly any amount of evidence would satisfy him as to the Gospel miracles. Thus running through the whole history of the conflict between Christianity and modern doubt the miracle is the *crux*. Somehow it must be gotten rid of, is the cry from every class, whether it be the Rationalist, quickly following the Deist in the order of succession; or the Pantheist, who deifies the universe in which God first knows himself in the self-consciousness of man; or the Positivist, who accounts for every thing by the operation of physical laws; or the Culturist, who accepts the known facts of man's condition, and dismissing all reference to God as the Unknowable, would, by a gospel of "sweetness and light," perfect human nature and usher in a reign which "maketh for righteousness."

The chief obstacle in getting rid of the miracle has been, and still is, Jesus the Christ. What will ye do then with Jesus? And the chief obstacle in getting rid of Christ is Christianity; Christianity not only as taught by Christ, but as developed in history, existing in the Church, and as it affects the face of civilization and the course of the world. Given Christianity, and it must have an adequate cause in the Christ. A system so replete with wisdom, power and benevolence, which saves its adherents from sin and makes them superior to death, must owe itself to one who was every way sufficient to produce it. Then given such a person as Christ, and the religion which emanates from him is as the sun's rays to the sun. Himself the Life, he can not but reproduce himself in living members, who shall share his nature and propagate that nature indefinitely. "Verily, verily, I say unto you, except a corn of wheat fall into the ground and die, it abideth alone; but if it die, it bringeth forth much fruit. And I, if I be lifted up from the earth, will draw all men unto me. This he said, signifying what death he should die." (John xii, 24, 32, 33.)

The whole argument for the character of Jesus might be rested, if necessary, upon this enunciation from his own lips of the law of love and self-surrender as the law of his life: and the results following his earthly existence need no other vindication as to their divinity, than as streams flowing from such a source. The so-called heroes of the world have conquered by shedding other men's blood; but this man by shedding *his own.* Indeed, whatever excellences the religions of the Old World possessed, and they had many, there was little or no place in them for sorrow and weakness. Their Jupiters and Minervas and Venuses might be cruel, revengeful, and deceitful, but they must not be weak, lacking either in physical strength or beauty, though morally deformed. Weakness was a misfortune, if not a crime; hence paganism built no hospitals for the insane and blind, it provided no asylums for the aged and the incurable. That a man was not strong enough to defend himself in the battle of life was reason sufficient that he should die. The vestal virgins, equally with emperors, senators, patricians, and plebeians, would vote for the death-thrust to be given to the hapless victim who chanced to fall beneath the brute force of his antagonist. It was left for Christ to introduce the new element of *compassion* to the world. In his cross he showed the heart of God. Henceforth the Godhead was associated with the lowly and the suffering. Christ loses himself—his honor, wealth, fame, riches, his life—that he might by his own sacrifice gain all who in the same spirit of self-surrender would unite themselves to him. This spirit of benevolence takes the place of the spirit of selfishness which dominated the Old World, and dominates the New until the spirit of Christ touches and transfigures it. The compassion of Jesus shows itself more, if possible, to the morally weak and wretched. He was the friend of sinners. Himself sinless, the very incarnation of holiness, he put himself into such close contact with the vile and sinful by the power of his sympathy, that he made the sinner's sin his own. Mankind can never fail to be moved by the consideration that he who was without sin, was made sin, that he might save sinners. This element of revelation reaches the fallen, guilty soul, when all else has failed. It does this, not by excusing or palliating sin as a mere weakness, but exposing its guilt and corruption through the light of perfect love and purity, it affects to penitence, and subdues by forgiving. Is it any wonder that there have always been those who would at any moment die for Christ? It is the same spirit in the disciple as in the Master.

The founder of a system may be judged by his system, and the system must be judged by its best specimens. To have given the world St. Paul is enough to attest the divinity of Christianity. Paul is an unanswerable argument for Christ. To have conquered one such mind and appropriated it, is a victory, the pæan of which sounds on through all the centuries. Not only the fact of his existence, character, and labors, which so marvelously illustrate the sacrificial zeal of Christ, but his writings as unimpeachable historical documents, carry us straight to the earthly scenes of Christ's life and to those of his first disciples. Under the full weight of a debt of gratitude to Jesus which this great apostle of the Gentiles felt, and was ever glad in life and in death to express, he could say: "But what things were gain to me, those I counted loss for Christ. Yea, doubtless, and I count all things but loss for the excellency of the knowledge of Christ Jesus my Lord." For Paul we may account, but for Jesus who shall account? Truly His character was altogether original, and original because at once divine and human. Himself the greatest of miracles as the God-man, miracles became his natural expression. To deny them, and the history of Christianity as the greatest of them, is to deny him.

And while Christianity moves forward in the ever-widening moral results of the Gospel upon the succeeding ages, men will continue to reverence and trust its divine Author. While it does for mankind what it does, they will not quickly abandon it. So long as the world feels the pangs of guilt, it will welcome the glad evangel of pardon; while it still wrestles with corruption, it will welcome the offer of cleansing; while it yet gropes amid the conflicting lights and shadows of this checkered scene of things, it will hail the guidance of a divine Providence; and while people everywhere are dying and dropping into the grave, we can not cease to rejoice in the blessed hope for ourselves and our dead, "I am the resurrection and the life: he that believeth in me, though he were dead, yet shall he live." Men may be temporarily drawn away by another gospel, which is not another; but upon maturer reflection, born it may be of the hours of sorrow, they will return to the more stable foundations of the truth as it is in Jesus.

This new edition of the Philosophy of the Plan of Salvation is fittingly placed among the books to be read and studied by the Chautauqua students. Few American books have had a wider circulation, and none in their sphere have done more solid and abiding good. Even within a day or two, one of the most cultivated ladies of our land, whose tongue and pen are doing so much to mold the thoughts and actions of her countrywomen, has expressed her great debt to it, as saving her from skepticism and assisting to settle her in the faith of Christ at a most critical period in her intellectual and religious development. Amid all the shiftings of thought in the never-ceasing conflict between light and darkness, this work must hold its ground. It will meet wants ever liable to recur, especially with advanced youth, in the history of religious inquiry.

CONTENTS.

CHAPTER I.

Man will worship—He will become assimilated to the Character of the Object that he worships—Character of Heathen Deities Defective and Earthly—From this Corrupting Worship Man has no Power to extricate himself, ... 25

CHAPTER II.

Concerning the Design and Necessity of the Bondage in Egypt, ... 42

CHAPTER III.

Concerning Miracles—Particularly the Miracles which accompanied the Deliverance of the Israelites from Bondage in Egypt, ... 47

CHAPTER IV.

Concerning what was Necessary as the First Step in the Process of Revelation, ... 59

CHAPTER V.

Concerning the Necessity of Affectionate Obedience to God, and the Manner of producing that Obedience in the Hearts of the Israelites, ... 63

CHAPTER VI.

Concerning the Design and Necessity of the Moral Law, ... 71

CHAPTER VII.

Concerning the Development of the Idea of Holiness, and its Transfer to Jehovah as an Attribute, . . . 77

CHAPTER VIII.

Concerning the Origin of the Ideas of Justice and Mercy and their Transfer to the Character of Jehovah, . . 88

CHAPTER IX.

Concerning the Transition from the Material System, by which Religious Ideas were conveyed through the Senses to the Spiritual System, in which Abstract Ideas were conveyed by Words and Parables, ... 101

CHAPTER X.

Concerning the Medium of conveying to Men Perfect Instruction in Doctrine and Duty, ... 109

CHAPTER XI.

Concerning Some of the Peculiar Proofs of the Messiahship of Christ, ... 115

CHAPTER XII.

Concerning the Condition in Life which it was Necessary the Messiah should assume, in Order to benefit the Human Family in the Greatest Degree, by his Example and Instructions, ... 121

CHAPTER XIII.

Concerning the Essential Principles which must, according to the Nature of Things, lie at the Foundation of the Instruction of Christ, ... 128

CHAPTER XIV.

Concerning Faith, as the Exercise through which Truth reaches and affects the Soul, ... 132

CHAPTER XV.

Concerning the Manifestations of God which would be necessary, under the New and Spiritual Dispensation, to produce in the Soul of Man Affectionate Obedience, ... 142

CHAPTER XVI.

Concerning the Influence of Faith in Christ upon the Moral Disposition and Moral Powers of the Soul, 181

CHAPTER XVII.

Concerning the Design and Importance of the Means of Grace—Prayer—Praise—Preaching, ... 203

CHAPTER XVIII.

Concerning the Agency of God in carrying on the Work of Redemption, and the Manner in which that Agency is exerted, ... 221

CHAPTER XIX.

Concerning the Practical Effects of the System as exemplified in Individual Cases, ... 227

SUPPLEMENTARY CHAPTER.

An Objective Revelation necessary, as a Means of the Moral Culture of Mankind, ... 239

General Introduction.

BY CALVIN E. STOWE, D. D.

We ask not that a man should come to an investigation of the evidences of the Christian revelation with a prejudgment in its favor; we ask only that there be no prejudice in the soul against it. It is only when a man looks through a glass which is perfectly clear and pure, that he sees things as they are; if the glass be in the least degree distorted or discolored, every object seen through it will necessarily partake of the distortion and discoloration. So our Savior teaches us, Matt. v, 22, 23. This is said expressly in regard to the blinding power of avarice in perverting the religious judgments (compare vs. 19, 20); and the same is true of every other forbidden state of mind and affection. When there is no mental or moral preoccupation averse to the Christian system, the surprising adaptations of this system to meet and relieve the wants and sorrows of man, constitute a species of evidence which is real and most convincing; some traits, which on a superficial view seemed unfavorable, on closer scrutiny are found to be among the strongest links in the chain of demonstration. Again, the mind may be in such a state that the clearest evidence of this kind will produce upon it no effect whatever. There is a voluntary and perfect unsusceptibility to any impression from it.

The idea which I wish to convey can probably be best illustrated by an example. We will suppose a shipwreck in which every soul perishes except two passengers, whom we will name Benignus and Contumax. With nothing saved but their lives, they are cast upon the rocky shore of a desert island, where there is no prospect to cheer the eye, and neither vegetable nor animal nor human habitation to give them hope of aid or sustenance.

The first emotions of Benignus, after struggling through the waves, are admiring gratitude to God for giving him his life, and a cheerful confidence that he who had aided him thus far, would not then leave him to perish. The first emotions of Contumax are murmuring regret that he has lost his voyage and lost his money, and is thrown upon a desolate coast with no immediate prospect of getting away. He wonders why such ill-luck should always happen to him; he is indignant that he was ever such a fool as to trust himself to the sea; he wonders he could not have had sense enough to remain at home.

Presently Benignus discovers in the rock, far above the reach of the waves, a spacious cavern, the entrance to which is protected by an artificial wall, and its sides pierced, evidently by a human hand, for the admission of light and air. Benignus is delighted; he immediately concludes that some benevolent individuals, or some paternal government, had provided this shelter on purpose for unfortunate mariners who might be shipwrecked on the inhospitable shore.

Contumax scorns any such inference; he can not see why benevolent people should wish to drive poor shipwrecked wretches into such a dismal hole in the rock, instead of providing them with a comfortable and pleasant home. Benignus reminds him that a house with windows and doors could not endure the storms of such a coast; and as no one would live there to take care of it, it would be continually out of repair, and far less comfortable than the cavern; and, therefore, the very nature of the shelter provided should be regarded as a striking proof, not only of the benevolence, but also of the wisdom of the provider. But Contumax is thinking of a handsome house in a green yard, filled with the shrubbery of a fine climate, and can not see a particle of either wisdom or benevolence in the rocky grotto. He, however, avails himself of the shelter for want of better.

Benignus soon finds, carefully stored away beyond the reach of damp, a tinder-box with all the necessary furnishing, and a quantity of dry fuel for making a fire. "See," says he joyfully to his companion, "another proof of the benevolent care of the provider of the cavern; here are all the materials for making a quick fire, of which we are so much in need."

"How do you know," replies Contumax, "that these things came here in that way? They probably belong to some poor wretch who has been shipwrecked before us, and found a chance to get away again, as I wish from my heart I could do." Benignus thinks that the great care with which they were put away out of the reach of injury is a sufficient indication that they were not left by one joyously hastening away, intent only on his own selfish interest, but must have been deposited there by some benevolent hand, for the express purpose of relieving the suffering; but Contumax cherishes no such romantic ideas.

Benignus, greatly delighted with what he has already discovered, makes further search in the cave, and finds plain and wholesome provisions, such as would not soon be injured, together with medicines and cordials; and also a supply of coarse but clean and warm clothing, carefully cased up so as to preserve them from all injury of wet or moth. "Now, says Benignus to his companion, "you certainly will be convinced that this place was provided by some benevolent hand on purpose for the shipwrecked. Here is evidence which can not be gainsaid." "We have more reason to apprehend," growls Contumax," "that we have fallen upon the haunts of pirates, who are now absent on their depredations, but will soon return to murder us." "Nay," replies Benignus, "these are not the spoils of pirates: here are neither jewels nor silks, here is no gold or silver— here are neither costly viands nor rich wines nor intoxicating brandies; and, besides, the things are laid away with much more care and scrupulous nicety than suits the wasteful and licentious habits of pirates."

"Well, at any rate," replies Contumax, "the donor must be a vulgar, stingy fellow, to put us off with such coarse food and raiment." "But you do not consider," says Benignus, "that these things must not be so costly as to tempt cupidity, since they can not be kept under lock and key—and besides, they are healthful and comfortable, and far better adapted to the condition of those most likely to need them, than if they had been of fine material; for twenty sailors suffer shipwreck, where one gentleman is subject to such a misfortune." The only reply which Contumax has to this is, to keep the thought well up in his own mind, "I am a gentleman, and not a sailor."

Contumax, however, does not hesitate to warm himself by the fire which Benignus has made of the materials found in the cave; he partakes largely and with great zest of the provisions and cordials, simple as they are; gladly lays aside his own wet and torn clothing, for the coarse but comfortable and dry raiment provided for him; and fixing himself in the most easy position he can devise, and as near the various comforts of the grotto as he can get, he is quite ready to enter upon an argument to any extent. He is a great reasoner, Contumax is. He can prove most philosophically that Benignus *can not prove* that there was any benevolent intention at all in any body in providing and furnishing that cavern—he can prove to a dead certainty that, for all which can be proved to the contrary, it might have been a mere accident, a blunder, a selfish enterprise; that nobody knows any thing about it; and he can account for it in twenty ways, without the least supposition of wisdom or benevolence, or any thing of the kind. The only thing he is certain of is, that he is in a miserable place; he thinks somebody is greatly to blame for putting him there, and is under decided obligation to get him safely away again.

What kind of reasoning can you apply to such a mind? What sort of evidence can such a man perceive or appreciate? What can he see in a pure light while his eyes are suffused with jaundice?

This character represents, and not unfairly, by far the largest class of skeptics, which exist in Christian lands.

There is in them all a tinge of disaffection, of misanthropy, or rather, of *theomisey*—if we may be allowed to coin a word, to express an idea which is often a reality, but which in our proper English tongue as yet has no name. This gives a dark shade to all their views of evidence, and prevents their seeing any decided proof in trains of reasoning which, in other states of mind, would have all the force of absolute demonstration.

The man who has long held raw brandy in his mouth can not immediately distinguish the taste of delicate wines; and he who has accustomed his soul to the unfeeling roughness of a godless style of thought, loses the delicacy of moral perception, which to the experienced Christian is the very organ by which he receives and appropriates evidence on moral and religious subjects.

All reflecting men, when they seriously contemplate their moral condition in this world, feel very much like shipwrecked sailors. In regard to this single point there is very little difference between the believer and the unbeliever—between Benignus and Contumax. But there is a great difference in their feelings in reference to their condition after it has been surveyed. The believer feels that he yet has much to thank God for; he feels real gratitude that his position is not still worse than it proves to be. The unbeliever, on the other hand, *when he knows God, glorifies him not as God, neither is he thankful; and as a necessary consequence, he becomes vain in his imagination, and his foolish heart is darkened.* He feels under no particular obligation to God; on the contrary, he rather thinks that God is under decided obligation to him, to treat him very well, and bring him easily and safely through the bad place into which he has thrown him.

In this state of mind he looks upon the divine arrangements actually made for his spiritual good, and, almost as a matter of course, he is dissatisfied. Such being the different state of mind of the two classes of persons, the facts of the Christian revelation, although substantially the same as they present themselves to both, yet produce very diverse and even opposite effects; to the believer establishing his faith, to the unbeliever confirming his skepticism; *to the one a savor of life unto life, to the other a savor of death unto death.*

Meanwhile, the most scornful unbeliever quietly

avails himself of all the incidental advantages which the Christian system brings, makes himself very comfortable with all the social improvements which it originates, and employs the mental culture which he himself owes to it, in strenuous exertions to disprove its intelligent and benevolent origin.

We will endeavor to show, in a few particulars, the different effects which the same aspects of revelation produce on the two different classes of mind under consideration.

To both, revelation presents itself as, in the main, very plain and homely in its garb. To the unbeliever, this is offensive, unworthy of God. He would have something more in accordance with the ambitious style of the little greatness of this world, for he has never learned that the *foolishness of God is wiser than men, and the weakness of God is stronger than men.* The believer understands that the greater part of God's children, for whom revelation is designed, are plain and homely people, that their souls are as precious as the souls of the proud and mighty, and in eternity may be altogether more elevated; and he knows if one can not perceive the real dignity and refinement of Scripture, it must be because his ideas of dignity and refinement are fictitious, and not natural.

Both the believer and the unbeliever see things in the Bible that are severe and rough. The destruction of Sodom, the stoning of the Sabbath-breaker, the extirpation of the Canaanites, are matters of fact in the eyes of both. But in this atmosphere, the philosophic infidel feels as uncomfortably as Contumax in the cave. The believer, however, reflects that since God does not choose to purify men by physical omnipotence, but by moral means and influences only, he must of course address each age by means adapted to the condition of each, and rough generations must be met with severe measures; just as Benignus sees that a cavern with loop-holes and guard-walls, instead of a house with doors and windows, is admirably fitted to a desolate and stormy coast.

Both understand that the vicious, the indolent, and the careless can not attain to correct views of revealed truth; for the truth is so revealed that labor, effort, care, and even energetic strugglings, are essential to the acquisition of religious knowledge in its purity. To the unbeliever this is all distasteful. He feels as if God were under obligations to make the way of salvation such that men would walk in it as a matter of course, without either effort or thought of their own; that all the means of salvation should not only be such that they can be used, but such that they can not be abused; that men should not only be able to find the way of life, but absolutely unable to lose it. The believer perceives at once the total unreasonableness of these demands, and their entire inconsistency with all the arrangements of nature. It would be as easy for God to cover the earth with railroads as with mountains, with canals as with rivers—to cause houses, all finished and furnished, to spring out of the ground as well as trees, and make the wheat-stalk bear a well-baked loaf of bread just as easily as the grain of wheat—and thus save men all the hard labor of toilsome traveling, of digging and building, of plowing and planting, of harvesting and grinding and baking. But has God done this? And what would man be good for if he had? So, in religion, what would a free agent be who had nothing to do? In all nature, that which can be used is susceptible also of abuse; that which can do good can be perverted also to evil. Why does not the infidel require, as proof of the wisdom and goodness of the God of nature, a kind of water that can quench his thirst and clean his skin and float his ships, but which will never on any occasion drown any body or make an inundation; a kind of grain that will refresh his grass, but never wet his hay; a kind of ax that will cut wood, but never penetrate the flesh of the wood-cutter; a kind of fire that will cook his food and warm him when he is cold, but can never burn him or reduce his dwelling to ashes? These demands are all quite as reasonable as those which the infidel makes as conditions of his ideal revelation, and the objections which are urged with so much confidence against the Bible, and gain so easy a reception among men, proceed on a principle which would be scouted and scorned by all the world as unspeakably ridiculous if applied to nature. The believer recognizes the God of the Bible and the God of nature as the same; and when he sees the same kind of analogies running through both, it confirms his faith instead of shaking it.

These illustrations might be pursued to almost any extent, at least until they had made a book much larger than the unpretending little volume which they are designed to introduce to the reader.

Having known something of this work from its inception to its completion, having witnessed with pleasure its remarkable success with the public, being confident that its influence must be good, and only good, in these times when philosophical skepticism and superstitious credulity are equally abundant and equally mischievous, I would gladly do whatever may be in my power to increase its circulation.

The argument itself, if not entirely original, is developed with a care, a consistency, and a thoroughness which can nowhere else be found, certainly in the same compass; and the whole style of thought from beginning to end shows it to be the author's own work, and not a thing which he has borrowed from others.

Such books add just so much to our stock of real intellectual wealth. They are like introducing into a community the gold and silver coins in full weight, instead of setting up a new bank on paper capital, and issuing paper.

The argument will always be entirely satisfactory to Benignus; and though Contumax may still continue to cavil, every one will see that caviling and refuting are two very different matters.

PHILOSOPHY

OF THE

PLAN OF SALVATION.

Chapter I.

INTRODUCTORY.

MAN WILL WORSHIP—HE WILL BECOME ASSIMILATED TO THE CHARACTER OF THE OBJECT THAT HE WORSHIPS—CHARACTER OF HEATHEN DEITIES DEFECTIVE AND UNHOLY—FROM THIS CORRUPTING WORSHIP MAN HAS NO POWER TO EXTRICATE HIMSELF.

THERE are three facts, each of them fully developed in the experience of the human family, a consideration of which will prepare the mind for the investigation which follows. When considered in their relation to each other, and in their bearing upon the moral interests of mankind, they will be seen to be of exceeding importance. We will adduce these facts, in connection with the statements and principles upon which they rest, and show how vital are the interests which depend upon them.

THE FIRST FACT STATED.

There is in the nature of man, or in the circumstances in which he is conditioned, *something* which leads him to recognize and worship a superior being. What that *something* is, is not important in our present inquiry; whether it be a constitutional instinct inwrought by the Maker; whether it be a deduction of universal reason, inferring a first cause from the things that are made; whether it be the effect of tradition, descending from the first worshipers, through all the tribes of the human family; whether any or all of these be the cause, the fact is the same—*Man is a religious being;* HE WILL WORSHIP.

In view of this propension of human nature, philosophers, in seeking a generic appellation for man, have denominated him a "*religious animal.*" The characteristic is true of him in whatever part of the world he may be found, and in whatever condition; and it has been true of him in all ages of which we have any record, either fabulous or authentic.

Navigators have, in a few instances, reported that isolated tribes of men, whom they visited, recognized the existence of no superior being; subsequent researches, however, have generally corrected the error, and, in all cases, when it has been supposed that a tribe of men was found believing in no god, the fact has been stated as an evidence of their degradation below the mass of their species, and of their approximation to the confines of brute nature. Of the whole family of man, existing in all ages, and scattered over the four quarters of the globe, and in the isles of the sea, there is scarcely one well-authenticated exception to the fact that, moved by an impulse of nature, or the force of circumstances, man worships something which he believes to be endowed with the attributes of a superior being.

THE SECOND FACT STATED.

The second fact, connected, as it is, by the nature of things, with the preceding, assumes the highest degree of importance. It may be stated in the following terms: *Man, by worshiping, becomes assimilated to the moral character of the object which he worships.* This is an invariable principle, operating with the certainty of cause and effect. The worshiper looks upon the character of the object which he worships as the standard of perfection. He therefore condemns every thing in himself which is unlike, and approves of every thing which is like that character. The tendency of this is to lead him to abandon every thing in himself, and in his course of life, which is condemned by the character and precepts of his god, and to conform himself to that standard which is approved by the same criterion. The worshiper desires the favor of the object worshiped, and this, reason dictates, can be obtained only by conformity to the will and the character of that object. To become assimilated to the image of the object worshiped must be the end of desire with the worshiper. His aspirations, therefore, every time he worships do, from the nature of the case, assimilate his character more and more to the model of the object that receives his homage.

To this fact the whole history of the idolatrous world bears testimony. Without an exception, the character of every nation and tribe of the human family has been formed and modified, in a great degree, by the character attributed to their gods.

From the history of idolatrous nations we will cite a number of familiar cases, confirmatory of the foregoing statement, that man becomes like the object of his worship.

A most striking instance is that of the Scythians, and other tribes of the Northmen, who subdued and finally annihilated the Roman power. Odin, Thor, and others of their supposed deities, were ideas of hero-kings, blood-thirsty and cruel, clothed with the attributes of deity, and worshiped. Their worship turned the milk of human kindness into gall in the bosoms of their votaries, and they seemed, like blood-hounds, to be possessed of a horrid delight when they were reveling in scenes of blood and slaughter. It being believed that one of their hero-gods, after destroying great numbers of the human race, destroyed himself, it hence became disreputable to die in bed, and those who did not meet death in battle frequently committed suicide, supposing that to die a natural death might exclude them from favor in the hall of Valhalla.

Among the gods of the Greeks and Romans there were some names, in the early ages of their history, to which some virtuous attributes were attached; but the conduct and character generally attributed to their gods were marked deeply with such traits as heroism, vengeance, caprice, and lust. In the later history of these nations their idolatry degenerated in character, and became a system of most debasing tendency.

The heroism fostered by idolatry was its least injurious influence. Pope's couplet, had he thrown a ray or two of light across the background of the dark picture, would have been a correct delineation of the character of Pagan idols—

"Gods partial, changeful, passionate, unjust;
Whose attributes were rage, revenge, and lust."

In some cases the most corrupt attributes of human nature, and even of brute nature, were attributed to objects of worship, and while men bowed down to them, they sunk themselves to the lowest depths of vice. The Egyptians might be named as an instance. The first patrons of the arts and sciences were bruteworshipers; and it is testified of them that bestiality, the lowest vice to which human nature can descend, was common amongst them. The paintings and sculpture of their divinities, in the mummy catacombs, are for the most part clusters of beasts, birds, reptiles, and flies, grouped together in the most disgusting and unnatural relations; a true indication that the minds of the worshipers were filled with ideas the most vile and unnatural.

The ancient Venus, as worshiped by almost all

the elder nations of antiquity, was a personification of lust. The deeds required to be done at her polluting fane, as acts of homage, ought not to be named.

In the best days of Corinth—"Corinth, the eye of Greece"—the most sacred persons in the city were prostitutes, consecrated to the worship of Venus. From this source she derived a large portion of her revenues. The consequence was that her inhabitants became proverbial for dissoluteness and treachery.

To the heathen divinities, especially those placed at the head of the catalogue as the superior gods, what theologians have called the physical attributes of deity—omnipotent and omnipresent power—were generally ascribed; but their moral character was always defective, and generally criminal. As one of the best instances in the whole mythology of the ancients, the Roman Jupiter might be cited. Had a medal been struck delineating the character of this best of the gods, on one side might have been engraved *Almightiness, Omnipresence, Justice;* and on the reverse, *Caprice, Vengeance, Lust.* Thus men clothed depraved or bestial deities with almighty power, and they became cruel, or corrupt, or bestial in their affections, by the reaction of the character worshiped upon the character of the worshiper. In the strong language of a recent writer, "They clothed beasts and depraved beings with the attribute of almightiness, and in effect they worshiped almighty beasts and devils." And the more they worshiped the more they resembled them.

These testimonies concerning the influence of idolatrous worship, and the character of the idols worshiped, are maintained by authorities which render doubt in relation to their credibility impossible. Upon this subject the wiser men among the Greeks and Romans have borne unequivocal testimony. Plato, in the second book of the Republic, speaks of the pernicious influence of the conduct attributed to the gods, and suggests that such histories should not be rehearsed in public, lest they should influence the youth to the commission of crimes. Aristotle advises that statues and paintings of the gods should exhibit no indecent scenes, *except in the temples of such divinities as, according to common opinion, preside over sensuality.** What an affecting testimony of the most discriminating mind among the heathen! asserting not only the turpitude of the prevailing idolatry, but sanctioning the sensuality of their debauched worship.

As Rome and Greece grew older, the infection of idolatry festered, until the body politic became one mass of moral disease. The state of things, in the later ages of these nations, is well stated by a late writer of the first authority.† "We should naturally suppose," says this writer, "that among so great a variety of gods, of religious actions, of sacred vows, at least some better feeling of the heart must have been excited; that at least some truly pious sentiment would have been awakened. But when we con-

---
* Aristot. Politica vii, 18; ed. Schneider.
† Tholuck on the Influence of Heathenism.

sider the character of this superstition, and the testimony of contemporaneous writers, such does not appear to have been the fact. Petronius's history of that period furnishes evidence that temples were frequented, altars crowned, and prayers offered to the gods, in order that they might render nights of unnatural lust agreeable; that they might favor acts of poisoning; that they might cause robberies and other crimes to prosper." In view of the abominations prevailing at this period, the moral Seneca exclaimed: "How great now is the madness of men! They lisp the most abominable of prayers; and if a man is found listening, they are silent. What a man ought not to hear, they do not blush to relate to the gods." Again says he, "If any one considers what things they do, and to what things they subject themselves, instead of decency, he will find indecency; instead of the honorable, the unworthy; instead of the rational, the insane!" Such was heathenism and its influence, in the most enlightened ages, according to the testimony of the best men of those times.

In relation to modern idolatry, the world is full of living witnesses of its corrupting tendency. We will cite in illustration a single case or two. The following is extracted from a public document, laid before Parliament, by H. Oakley, Esq., a magistrate in lower Bengal. Speaking of the influence of idolatry in India, he says of the worship of Kalé, one of the most popular idols: "The murderer, the robber, and the prostitute, all aim to propitiate a being whose worship is obscenity, and who delights in the blood of man and beast; and, without imploring whose aid, no act of wickedness is committed. The worship of Kalé must harden the hearts of her followers; and to them scenes of blood and crime must become familiar."

In China, according to Medhurst, the priests of Buddha understand and teach the doctrine of the assimilation of the worshiper to the object worshiped. They say: "Think of Buddha and you will be transformed into Buddha. If men pray to Buddha and do not become Buddha, it is because the mouth prays, and not the mind." *

Two facts, then, are philosophically and historically true: First. Man is a religious animal, and will worship something as a superior being. Second. By worshiping, he becomes assimilated to the moral character of the object which he worships. And (the God of the Bible out of view for the present) those objects have always had a defective and unholy character.

Here, then, is one great source which has developed the corruption of the family of man. We inquire not in this place concerning the origin of idolatry: whatever, or wherever was its origin, its influence has been uniformly the same. As no object of idolatrous worship was ever conceived to be per-

---

* For a succinct statement of the universal prevalence of false religions, and their corrupting influence, see Ryan on the Effect of Religion upon Mankind, *passim*.

fectly just and benevolent, but most of them no better than the apotheosis of heroes, or the deification of the imperfect faculties and impure passions of human or brute nature, the result followed, with a certainty as unerring as cause and effect, that man, by following his instinct to worship, would becloud his intellect and corrupt his heart. Notice how inevitable, from the circumstances of the case, was the corruption of man's powers: he was led to worship by an instinct over which he had no control. The objects of his worship were, whether he originated them or not, all of them of a character that corrupted his heart; thus the gratification of his instinctive propensities inevitably strengthened the corruption of his nature.

Now, it is not our design to inquire whether, or how far, man was guilty in producing this evil condition of things. In view of the *facts* in the case the inquiry which forces itself upon the mind is: Were there any resources in human nature, or any means of any kind, of which man could avail himself by which he might save himself from the debasing influence of idolatrous worship? In reply,

THE THIRD FACT IS STATED.

There were no means within the reach of human power or wisdom, by which man could extricate himself from the evil of idolatry, either by an immediate or by a progressive series of efforts.

This fact is maintained from the history of idolatry, the testimony of the heathen philosophers, and the nature of man.

1. Instead of man acquiring the power or the disposition, as the race became older, to destroy idolatry, idolatry, from its first inception in the world, gained power to destroy him. Amid all the mutations of society, from barbarous to civilized, and amid all the conflicts of nations and the changes of dynasties and forms of government, from the first historic notices which we have of the human family down to the era of Christ, idolatry constantly became more evil in its character and more extended in its influence. It is well ascertained that the first objects of idolatrous homage were few and simple, and the worship of the earliest ages comparatively pure. Man fell into this moral debasement but one step at a time. The sun, moon, stars, and other conspicuous objects of creative power and wisdom, received the first idolatrous homage. Afterwards a divinity was supposed to reside in other objects, especially in those men, and beasts, and things, which were instrumental in conferring particular benefits on tribes or nations of men. And finally, images of those objects were formed and worshiped. Images, which subsequently became innumerable, were not so in the earliest historic ages. In some nations they were not allowed until after the era of the foundation of Rome.* As the nations grew older, images, which were at the first but few and clothed with drapery,

---

* Plutarch says that Numa forbade the Romans to make statues of their gods.

became more numerous, and were presented before the worshipers in a state of nudity, and in the most obscene attitudes. And as has been before stated, their character, from being comparatively innoxious, became, without exception, demoralizing in the extreme.

2. During the Augustan age of Rome, and the age of Pericles and Alcibiades in Greece—those periods when the mind had attained the highest elevation ever known among heathen nations—the mass of the people were more idolatrous in their habits, and consequently more corrupt in their hearts, than ever before. The abominations of idol-worship, of the mysteries, and of lewdness, in forms too vile to name, were rife throughout the country and the villages, and had their foci in the capitals of Greece and Rome. Jahn says, in relation to this period: "Deities increased in number, and the apotheosis of vicious emperors was not unfrequent. Their philosophers, indeed, disputed with much subtlety respecting the architect of the universe, but they knew nothing about the Creator, the holy and almighty Judge of men."

Some of the more intelligent of the philosophers, perceiving the evil of the prevailing idolatry, desired to refine the grossness of the popular faith. They taught that the facts believed concerning the gods were allegories. Some endeavored to identify the character of some of their deities with the natural virtues; while many of them became skeptical concerning the existence of the gods and of a future state. Those were, however, but isolated exceptions to the mass of mankind. And, had their views been adopted by others, they would only have modified, not remedied the evil. But a contemporary writer shows how entirely unavailing, even to modify the evil, was the teaching of the philosophers. Dionysius of Halicarnassus says: "There are only a few who have become masters of this philosophy. On the other hand, the great and unphilosophic mass are accustomed to receive these narratives rather in their worst sense, and to learn one of these two things, either to despise the gods as beings who wallow in the grossest licentiousness, or not to restrain themselves even from what is most abominable and abandoned, when they see that the gods do the same." Cicero, in one sentence, as given by Tholuck, notices both the evil and its cause; confirming, in direct language, the preceding views. "Instead," says he, "of the transfer to man of that which is divine, they transferred human sins to the gods, and then experienced again the necessary reaction." Such, then, is the testimony of the philosophers in relation to the idolatry of their times. A few gifted individuals obtained sufficient light to see the moral evil in which men were involved, but they had neither wisdom to devise a remedy, nor power to arrest the progress of the moral pestilence that was corrupting the noble faculties of the human soul.

3. It was impossible, from the nature of man, that he should extricate himself from the corrupting influence of idolatry. In this place we wish to state a

principle which should be kept in view throughout the following discussion: *If man were ever redeemed from idolatrous worship, his redemption would have to be accomplished by means and instrumentalities adapted to his nature and the circumstances in which he existed.* If the faculties of his nature were changed, he would not be man. If his temporal condition were changed, different means would be necessary. If, therefore, man, *as man*, in his present condition, were to be recovered, the means of recovery, whether instituted by God or man, must be adapted to his nature and his circumstances.

The only way, then, in which relief was possible for man was that an object of worship should be placed before the mind directly opposite in moral character to those he had before adored. If his heart was ever purified, it must be by tearing his affections from his gods, and fixing them upon a righteous and holy being as the proper object of his homage. But for man to form such an object was plainly impossible. He could not transfer a better character to his gods than he himself possessed. Man could not "bring a pure thing out of an impure." The effect could not rise higher in moral purity than the cause. Human nature, in the maturity of its faculties, all agree, is imperfect and selfish; and for an imperfect and selfish being to originate a perfect and holy character, deify it, and worship it, is to suppose what is contrary to the nature of things. The thought of the eloquent and philosophic Cicero expresses all that man could do. He could transfer his own imperfect attributes to the gods, and, by worshiping a being characterized by these imperfections, he would receive in himself the reaction of his own depravity.

But if some men had had the power and the disposition to form for the world a perfectly holy object of worship, still the great difficulty, as we have seen in the case of the philosophers, would have remained; that is, a want of the necessary power to arrest the progress of idolatry and substitute the better worship. To doubt the truth of the prevailing idolatry was all that men, at the highest intellectual attainment ever acquired in heathen countries, could do. And, if they had had power to convey their doubts to all minds in all the world, it would only have been to place mankind in the chaotic darkness of atheism, and leave them to be led again by their instincts into the abominations of imperfect and impure worship.

The testimony, then, is conclusive, from the history of idolatry, that the evil became greater every age—from the statements of the wisest of the heathen, that they had no power to arrest its progress, and from the nature of man, that it was not possible for him to relieve himself from the corrupting influence of idolatry, in which he had become involved.

From the foregoing facts and reasonings, it is plain that the high-born faculties of the human soul must have been blighted forever by a corrupting worship, unless two things were accomplished; neither of which it was in the power of human nature to effect; and yet both of which were essentially necessary to accomplish the elevation of man from the pit into which he had fallen.

The first thing necessary to be accomplished was that *a pure object of worship should be placed before the eye of the soul.* Purity of heart and conscience would be necessary in the object of worship, otherwise the heart and conscience of the worshiper would not be purified. But if an object were presented whose nature was infinitely opposed to sin—to all defilement, both physical and spiritual—and who revealed, in his example and by his precepts, a perfect standard to govern the life of man under the circumstances in which he was placed, then man's mind would be enlightened, his conscience rectified, and the hard and corrupt feelings of his heart softened and purified, by assimilation to the object of his worship. As, according to the nature of things, an unholy object of worship would necessarily degrade and corrupt the human soul, so, on the contrary, a holy object worshiped would necessarily elevate and purify the nature of man.

The second necessary thing in order to man's redemption was, *that when a holy object of worship was revealed, the revelation should be accompanied with sufficient power to influence men to forsake their former worship, and to worship the holy object made known to them.* The presentation of a new and pure object would not cause men to turn from their former opinions and practices, and become directly opposed in heart to what they had formerly loved. A display of power would be necessary, sufficient to overcome their former faith and their present fears, and to detach their affections from idols, and fix them upon the proper object of human homage.

It follows, then, that man must remain a corrupt idolater forever, unless God interpose in his behalf. The question whether he would thus interpose, in the only way possible, to save the race from moral death, depends entirely upon the benevolence of his nature. The question whether he *has* done so may be answered by inquiring whether any system of means has been instituted in the world, characterized by sufficient power to destroy idolatry, revealing at the same time a holy object of worship; and this revelation being accompanied by means and influence so adapted to man's nature as to secure the result.

To this inquiry the future pages of this volume will be devoted. The inquiry is not primarily concerning the truth of the Bible, but concerning the only religion possible for mankind, and the only means by which such religion could be given consistently with man's nature and circumstances.

Chapter II.

CONCERNING THE DESIGN AND NECESSITY OF THE BONDAGE IN EGYPT.

There are certain bonds of union and sources of sympathy by which the minds of a whole people may be united into one common mind; so much so, that all hearts in the nation will be affected by the same subjects, and all minds moved by the same motives. Any cause which creates a common interest and a common feeling, common biases and common hopes, in the individual minds which compose a nation, has a tendency to unite them in this manner.

Some of the causes which have more power than any others to bind men, as it were, into a common being, are the following: The natural tie of consanguinity, or a common parentage, is a strong bond of affiliation among men. And there are others which, in some cases, seem to be even stronger than this: among these may be named a common interest; a common religion; and a common fellowship in suffering and deliverance. Any circumstance which educes the susceptibilities of the mind and twines them together, or around a common object; any event in which the interest, the feelings, the safety, or the reputation of any people is involved, causes them to be

more closely allied to each other in social and civil compact.

The more firmly a people are bound together by these ties of union, the more strength they will possess to resist opposing interests and opinions from without; while, at the same time, every thing national, or peculiar to them as a people, will be cherished with warmer and more tenacious attachment.

From the operation of this principle originates the maxim, "*Union is strength;*" and whether the conflict be mental or physical, the people who are united together by the most numerous and powerful sympathies will oppose the strongest and the longest resistance to the innovations of external forces. On the contrary, if the bonds of moral union are few and easily sundered, the strength of the nation is soon broken, and the fragments easily repelled from each other.

According to this principle, in all cases in which a whole nation are to be instructed, or prepared for offense and defense, or in any wise fitted to be acted upon, or to act as a nation, it would be necessary that the bonds of national union should be numerous and strong, and that as far as possible a perfect oneness of interest and feeling should pervade the nation.

So long as the human mind and human circumstances continue what they are, no power in heaven or on earth could unite a people together, except by the same or similar means as have been stated. If, therefore, God designed to form a nation, either to be acted upon or to act as a nation, he would put in operation those agencies which would bind them firmly and permanently into one mass.

Now, mark the application of these deductions to the case of the Israelites. About the period when the corruptions of idolatry were becoming generally prevalent, Abraham, the Bible record states, was extricated by divine interposition. He was assured that his descendants should suffer a long bondage, and afterwards become a numerous nation. Abraham was their common ancestor, one whom they remembered with reverence and pride; and each individual felt himself honored by the fact that the blood of the "Father of the faithful" circled in his veins. The tie of consanguinity in their case was bound in the strongest manner, and encircled the whole nation. In Egypt their circumstances and employments were the same; and in the endurance of a protracted and most galling bondage they had a common lot. Their liberation was likewise a national deliverance, which affected alike the whole people, the anniversary of which was celebrated by distant posterity with strong and peculiar national enthusiasm.

Now, it has been said that the events of our colonial servitude, and the achievement of American independence, are points in our history which will ever operate upon our national character, impressing clear views of the great principles of Republicanism, and uniting all hearts in support of those principles: how much more affecting and indelible, then, was the impress made upon the national heart of the Israelites by their bondage and deliverance! They were bound by blood, by interest, feeling, hopes, fears, by bondage and by faith.

And how firmly did these providences weave into one web the sympathies and views of the Jewish people! It is a fact which is the miracle of history, and the wonder of the world, that the ties which unite this people seem to be indissoluble. While other nations have risen and reigned and fallen; while the ties which united them have been sundered, and their fragments lost amid earth's teeming population, the stock of Abraham endures, like an incorruptible monument of gold, undestroyed by the attrition of the waves of time, which have dashed in pieces and washed away other. nations, whose origin was but yesterday compared with this ancient and wonderful people.

In this manner was this nation prepared for peculiar duties, and to discharge those duties under peculiar circumstances. Many of the nations by which they were surrounded were more powerful than themselves; all were warlike, and each had its peculiar system of idolatry, which corrupted all hearts that came within its influence. Hence the necessity that this people should be so united together as to resist the power and contagious example of surrounding nations, while they were fitted to receive and preserve a peculiar national character, civil polity, and religious doctrines; of all which they were to be the conservators amid surrounding and opposing heathenism, for many ages.

Other items might be added to the induction which

would make the design, if possible, more apparent. If the Jews were to be the recipients of new instruction, to obey new laws, and to sustain new institutions, it would be desirable that their minds, so far as possible, should be in the condition of new material, occupied by little previous knowledge, and by no national prejudices against or in favor of governmental forms and systems. Now, in the case of the Jews, the habit of obedience had been acquired. They had no national predilections or prejudices arising from past experience. In relation to knowledge of any kind, their mind was almost a *tabula rasa*. They were as new material prepared to receive the molding of a master hand and the impress of a governing mind.

Now, as this discipline of the descendants of Abraham was the result of a long concatenation of events, and could not have been designed by themselves to accomplish the necessary end; and as the whole chain of events was connected together and perfectly adapted, in accordance with the nature of things, to produce the specific purpose which was accomplished by them, it follows as the only rational conclusion, first, that the overruling intelligence of God was employed in thus preparing material for a purer religious worship than the world then enjoyed; and, second, that a nation could have been so prepared by no other agent, and in no other way.

Chapter III.

CONCERNING MIRACLES — PARTICULARLY THE MIRACLES WHICH ACCOMPANIED THE DELIVERANCE OF THE ISRAELITES FROM BONDAGE IN EGYPT.

THERE has been so much false philosophy written concerning the subject of miracles, that it is difficult for those conversant with the speculations of writers upon this subject to divest their minds sufficiently of preformed biases to examine candidly the simple and natural principles upon which is based the evidence and necessity of miraculous interposition.

The following statement is true beyond controversy: *Man can not, in the present constitution of his mind, believe that religion has a divine origin unless it be accompanied with miracles.* The necessary inference of the mind is, that if an Infinite Being acts, his acts will be superhuman in their character; because the effect, reason dictates, will be characterized by the nature of its cause. Man has the same reason to expect that God will perform acts above human power and knowledge that he has to suppose the inferior orders of animals will, in their actions, sink below the power and wisdom which characterizes human nature. For as it is *natural* for man to perform acts superior to the power and knowledge of the animals beneath him, so reason affirms that it is *natural* for God to develop his power by means and in ways above the skill and ability of mortals. Hence, if God manifest himself at all—unless, in accommodation to the capacities of men, he should constrain his manifestations within the compass of human ability—every act of God's immediate power would, to human capacity, be a miracle. But if God were to constrain all his acts within the limits of human means and agencies, it would be impossible for man to discriminate between the acts of the Godhead and the acts of the manhood. And man, if he considered acts of a divine origin which were plainly within the compass of human ability, would violate his own reason.

Suppose, for illustration, that God desired to reveal a religion to men, and wished them to recognize his character and his benevolence in giving that revelation. Suppose, further, that God should give such a revelation, and that every appearance and every act connected with its introduction was characterized by nothing superior to human power. Could any rational mind on earth believe that such a system of religion came from God? Impossible! A man could as easily be made to believe that his own child, who possessed his own lineaments and his own nature, belonged to some other world and some other order of the creation. It would not be possible for God to convince men that a religion was from heaven, unless it was accompanied with the marks of divine power.

Suppose, again, that some individual were to appear either in the heathen or Christian world—he claimed to be a teacher sent from God, yet aspired to the performance of no miracles; he assumed to do nothing superior to the wisdom and ability of other men. Such an individual, although he might succeed in gaining proselytes to some particular view of a religion already believed, yet he could never make men believe that he had a special commission from God to establish a new religion, for the simple reason that he had no grounds more than his fellows to support his claims as an agent of the Almighty. But if he could convince a single individual that he had wrought a miracle, or that he had power to do so, that moment his claims would be established, in that mind, as a commissioned agent from heaven. So certainly, and so intuitively, do the minds of men revere and expect miracles as the credentials of the divine presence.

This demand of the mind for miracles, as testimony of the divine presence and power, is intuitive with all men; and those very individuals who have doubted the existence or necessity of miracles, should they examine their own convictions on this subject, would see that by an absolute necessity, if they desired to give the world a system of religion, whether truth or imposture, in order to make men receive it as of divine authority, they must work miracles to attest its truth, or make men believe that they did so. Men can produce doubt of a revelation in no way until they have destroyed the evidence of its miracles; nor can faith be produced in the divine origin of a religion until the evidence of miracles is supplied.

The conviction that miracles are the true attestation of immediate divine agency is so constitutional (allow the expression) with the reason, that so soon as men persuade themselves they are the special agents of God in propagating some particular truth in the world, they adopt likewise the belief that they have ability to work miracles. There have been many sincere enthusiasts, who believed that they were special agents of heaven, and in such cases the conviction of their own miraculous powers arises as a necessary concomitant of the other opinion. Among such, in modern times, may be instanced Immanuel Swedenborg, and Irving, the Scotch preacher. Impostors also, perceiving that miracles were necessary in order that the human mind should receive a religion as divine, have invariably claimed miraculous powers. Such instances recur constantly from the days of Elymas down to the Mormon, Joseph Smith.

All the multitude of false religions, that have been believed since the world began, have been introduced by the power of this principle. MIRACLES BELIEVED, lie at the foundation of all religions which men have ever received as of divine origin. No matter how degrading or repulsive to reason in other respects, the fact of its establishment and propagation grows out of the belief of men that miraculous agency lies at the bottom. This belief will give currency to any system, however absurd, and without it no system can be established in the minds of men, however high and holy may be its origin and its design.

Such, then, is the constitution which the Maker has given to the mind. Whether the conviction be an intuition or an induction of the reason, God is the primary cause of its existence; and its existence puts it out of the power of man to receive a revelation from God himself, unless accompanied with miraculous manifestations. If, therefore, God ever gave a revelation to man, it was necessarily accompanied with miracles, and with miracles of such a nature as would clearly distinguish the divine character and the divine authority of the dispensation.

The whole fullness and force of these deductions apply to the case of the Israelites. The laws of their mind not only demanded miracles as an attestation of divine interposition; but at that time the belief existed in their minds that miracles were constantly performed. Although they remembered the God of Abraham, Isaac, and Jacob, yet they likewise, as subsequent facts clearly attested, believed that the idols of Egypt possessed the attributes of divinity. The belief in a plurality of gods was then common to all nations. And although this error was corrected, and perhaps entirely removed, by succeeding providences and instructions, from the minds of the Jews, yet before the miracles in Egypt, while the God of Abraham was, perhaps, in most cases acknowledged as their God, the idols of Egypt were acknowledged as the gods of the Egyptians, and probably worshiped as the divinities who had power to dispense good and evil to all the inhabitants of that land. And, in common with all Egypt, they, no doubt, believed that the acts of jugglery, in which the magicians or priests of Egypt had made astonishing proficiency, were actual miracles, exhibiting the power of their idols, and the authority of the priests to act in their name.

In view, therefore, of existing circumstances, two things were necessary, on the part of God,[*] in order to give any revelation to the Israelites: First, that he should manifest himself by miracles; and second, that those miracles should be of such a character as evidently to distinguish them from the jugglery of the magicians, and to convince all observers of the existence and omnipotence of the true God, in contradistinction from the objects of idolatrous worship. Unless these two things were done, it would have been impossible for the Israelites to have recognized JEHOVAH as the *only living* and *true* GOD.

It follows, then, that by the miracles which God wrought by the hand of Moses, he pursued the only way that was possible to give a revelation in which his presence and power would be recognized. The only point of inquiry remaining is, Were the miracles of such a character and performed in such a manner as to remove false views from the minds of the Israelites, and to introduce right views concerning the true God and the non-existence of factitious objects of worship?

---

[*] When we speak of a thing as necessary on the part of God, it is said, not in view of God's attributes, but in view of man's nature and circumstances.

PLAN OF SALVATION. 53

With this point in view, the design in the management and character of the miracles in Egypt is interesting and obvious. Notice, first, the whole strength of the magicians' skill was brought out and measured with that of the miraculous power exerted through Moses. If this had not been done, the idea would have remained in the minds of the people, that although Moses wielded a mighty, miraculous power, it might be derived from the Egyptian gods; or if it was not thus derived, they might have supposed that if the priests of those idols were summoned they could contravene or arrest the power vested in Moses by Jehovah. But now, the magicians appearing in the name of their gods, the power of Moses was seen to be not only superior to their sorceries, but hostile to them and their idolatrous worship.

Notice, second, the design and adaptedness of the miracles, not only to distinguish the power of the true God, but to destroy the confidence placed in the protection and power of the idols.

The first miracle, while it authenticated the mission of Moses, destroyed the serpents, which among the Egyptians were objects of worship; thus evincing, in the outset, that their gods could neither help the people nor save themselves.

The second miracle was directed against the river Nile, another object which they regarded with religious reverence. This river they held sacred, as the Hindoos do the Ganges; and even the fish in its waters they revered as objects of worship. They drank the water with reverence and delight, and supposed that a divine efficacy dwelt in its waves to heal diseases of the body. The water of this their cherished object of idolatrous homage was transmuted to blood; and its finny idols became a mass of putridity.

The third miracle was directed to the accomplishment of the same end, the destruction of faith in the river as an object of worship. The waters of the Nile were caused to send forth legions of frogs, which infested the whole land, and became a nuisance and a torment to the people. Thus their idol, by the power of the true God, was polluted and turned into a source of pollution to its worshipers.

By the fourth miracle of a series constantly increasing in power and severity, lice came upon man and beast throughout the land. "Now, if it be remembered," says Gleig, "that no one could approach the altars of Egypt upon whom so impure an insect harbored; and that the priests, to guard against the slightest risk of contamination, wore only linen garments, and shaved their heads and bodies every day,* the severity of this miracle as a judgment upon Egyptian idolatry may be imagined. Whilst it lasted no act of worship could be performed, and so keenly was this felt that the very magicians exclaimed, "This is the finger of God."

The fifth miracle was designed to destroy the trust of the people in Beelzebub, or the Fly-god, who was

---

* Every third day according to Herodotus.

reverenced as their protector from visitations of swarms of ravenous flies, which infested the land generally about the time of the dog-days, and removed only, as they supposed, at the will of this idol. The miracle now wrought by Moses evinced the impotence of Beelzebub, and caused the people to look elsewhere for relief from the fearful visitation under which they were suffering.

The sixth miracle, which destroyed the cattle, excepting those of the Israelites, was aimed at the destruction of the entire system of brute worship. This system, degrading and bestial as it was, had become a monster of many heads in Egypt. They had their sacred bull, and ram, and heifer, and goat, and many others, all of which were destroyed by the agency of the God of Moses. Thus, by one act of power, Jehovah manifested his own supremacy, and destroyed the very existence of their brute idols.

Of the peculiar fitness of the sixth plague (the seventh miracle), says the writer before quoted, the reader will receive a better impression, when he is reminded that in Egypt there were several altars upon which human sacrifices were occasionally offered, when they desired to propitiate Typhon, or the Evil Principle. These victims being burned alive, their ashes were gathered together by the officiating priests, and thrown up into the air, in order that evil might be averted from every place to which an atom of the ashes was wafted. By the direction of Jehovah, Moses took a handful of ashes from the furnace (which, very probably, the Egyptions at this time had frequently used to turn aside the plagues with which they were smitten), and he cast it into the air, as they were accustomed to do; and instead of averting evil, boils and blains fell upon all the people of the land. Neither king, nor priest, nor people escaped. Thus the bloody rites of Typhon became a curse to the idolators, the supremacy of Jehovah was affirmed, and the deliverence of the Israelites insisted upon.

The ninth miracle was directed against the worship of Serapis, whose peculiar office was supposed to be to protect the country from locusts. At periods these destructive insects came in clouds upon the land, and, like an overshadowing curse, they blighted the fruits of the field and the verdure of the forest. At the command of Moses these terrible insects came, and they retired only at his bidding. Thus was the impotence of Serapis made manifest, and the idolators taught the folly of trusting in any other protection than that of Jehovah, the God of Israel.

The eighth and tenth miracles were directed against the worship of Isis and Osiris, to whom and the river Nile they awarded the first place* in the long catalogue of their idolatry. These idols were originally the representatives of the sun and moon; they were

---

* Against the worship of the Nile two miracles were directed, and two likewise against Isis and Osiris, because they were supposed to be the supreme gods. Many placed the Nile first, as they said it had power to water Egypt independently of the action of the elements.

believed to control the light and the elements; and their worship prevailed in some form among all the early nations. The miracles directed against the worship of Isis and Osiris must have made a deep impression on the minds both of the Israelites and the Egyptians. In a country where rain seldom falls, where the atmosphere is always calm, and the light of the heavenly bodies always continued, what was the horror pervading all minds during the elemental war described in the Hebrew record; during the long period of three days and three nights, while the gloom of thick darkness settled, like the outspread pall of death, over the whole land! Jehovah of Hosts summoned Nature to proclaim him the true God; the God of Israel asserted his supremacy, and exerted his power to degrade the idols, destroy idolatry, and liberate the descendants of Abraham from the land of their bondage.

The Almighty having thus revealed himself as the true God by miraculous agency, and pursued those measures, in the exercise of his power, which were directly adapted to destroy the various forms of idolatry which existed in Egypt, the eleventh and last miracle was a judgment, in order to manifest to all minds that Jehovah was the God who executes judgment in the earth.

The Egyptians had for a long time cruelly oppressed the Israelites, and to put the finishing horror to their atrocities they had finally slain at their birth the offspring of their victims; and now God, in the exercise of infinite justice, visited them with righteous retribution. In the mid-watches of the night the "Angel of the Pestilence" was sent to the dwellings of Egypt, and he "breathed in the face" of all the first-born in the land. In the morning, the hope of every family, from the palace to the cottage, was a corpse. What mind can imagine the awful consternation of that scene, when an agonizing wail rose from the stricken hearts of all the parents in the nation! The cruel task-masters were taught, by means which entered their souls, that the true God was a God not only of power, but of judgment, and as such to be feared by evil-doers and reverenced by those that do well.

The demonstration, therefore, is conclusive that in view of the idolatrous state of the world, and especially in view of the character and circumstances of the Israelites, the true God could have made a revelation of himself in no other way than by the means and in the manner of the miracles of Egypt; and none but the true God could have revealed himself in this way.*

---

*In accordance with the foregoing are the intimations given in the Bible of the design of the miracles of Egypt. By these exhibitions of divine power God said, "Ye," the Israelites, "and Pharaoh shall know that I am Jehovah." Miracles, moreover, was the evidence that Pharaoh required. Ex. vii, 9, God said to Moses that when he should present himself as the divine legate, and Pharaoh should require a miracle, to perform it accordingly.

In relation to the destruction of idolatry, the design of Jehovah is expressly announced, Ex. xii, 12: "Against all the gods of Egypt will I execute judgment; I am Jehovah." See also Ex. xviii, 11.

Chapter IV.

CONCERNING WHAT WAS NECESSARY AS THE FIRST STEP IN THE PROCESS OF REVELATION.

By the miracles of Egypt the false views and corrupt habits of the Israelites were, for the time being, in a great measure removed. Previously they had believed in a plurality of gods; and although they remembered the God of Abraham, yet they had, as is evident from notices in the Bible, associated with his attribute of almighty power (the only attribute well understood by the Patriarchs) many of the corrupt attributes of the Egyptian idols. Thus the idea of God was debased by having groveling and corrupt attributes superinduced upon it. By miraculous agency these dishonorable views of the divine character were removed; their minds were emptied of false impressions in order that they might be furnished with the true idea and the true attributes of the Supreme Being.

But how could minds in the infancy of knowledge respecting God and human duty, having all they had previously learned removed, and being now about to take the first step in their progress—how could the first principles of divine knowledge be conveyed to such minds?

One thing in the outset would evidently be necessary: knowledge, as the mind is constituted, can be communicated in no other way than progressively; it would be necessary, therefore, that they should begin with the elementary principles, and proceed through all the stages of their education. The mind can not receive at once all the parts of a system in religion, science, or any other department of human knowledge. One fact or idea must be predicated upon another, just as one stone rests upon another, from the foundation to the top of the building. There are successive steps in the acquisition of knowledge, and every step in the mind's progress must be taken from advances already made. God has inwrought the law of progression into the nature of things, and observes it in his own works. From the springing of a blade to the formation of the mind, or of a world, every thing goes forward by consecutive steps.

It was necessary, therefore, in view of the established laws of the mind, that the knowledge of God and human duty should be imparted to the Israelites by successive communications; necessary that there should be a first step, or primary principle, for a starting point, and then a progression onward and upward to perfection.

In accordance with these principles, God, in the introduction of the Mosaic dispensation, revealed only his essential existence to the Israelites. In Exodus iii, 13, 14, it is stated that Moses inquired of God, "Behold, when I come unto the children of Israel and say unto them, The God of your fathers hath sent me unto you, and they shall say unto me, What is his name? what shall I say unto them? And God said, I am THE I AM; and he said, Thus shalt thou say unto the children of Israel, I AM hath sent me unto you." In the Hebrew text the simple form of the verb is used, corresponding with the first person present, indicative, of the English verb *to be*—simply, "I am," conveying no idea but that of personality and existence. WHAT he was, besides his existence thus revealed, was afterwards to be learned. This was a revelation of divine BEING, a nucleus of essential deity, as a foundation fact of the then new dispensation, upon which God, by future manifestations, might engraft the attributes of his nature.

Thus, at the outset of the dispensation there was thrown into their minds a first truth. God revealed his divine existence; and the idea of God, thus revealed, was in their minds, without any other attribute being connected with it than that of infinite power— an attribute of the Godhead which all men derive from the works of nature—which was known to the Patriarchs as belonging to the true God, and which was now, by the miracles manifesting supreme power, appropriated to I AM—Jehovah—the God of the Israelites.

Thus were this peculiar people carried back to the first principles of natural religion, their mind disembarrassed from false notions previously entertained, and the true idea of the supreme God and Judge of men revealed. By these providences they were prepared, in a manner consistent with the nature of things and the nature of mind, to receive a further revelation of the moral attributes of Jehovah, whom they now recognized as the Supreme God.

Chapter V.

CONCERNING THE NECESSITY OF AFFECTIONATE OBEDIENCE TO GOD; AND THE MANNER OF PRODUCING THAT OBEDIENCE IN THE HEARTS OF THE ISRAELITES.

The following principles in relation to the affections will be recognized by consciousness as true in the experience of every man. As they lie at the foundation of the moral exercises of the soul, and as they relate to the sources and central principles of all true religion, it will be necessary for the reader to notice them, in order that he may see their application in subsequent pages.

1. The affections of the soul move in view of certain objects, or in view of certain qualities believed to exist in those objects. The affections never move—in familiar words, the heart never loves—unless love be produced by seeing, or *by believing that we see* some lovely and excellent qualities in the object. When the soul believes those good qualities to be possessed by another, and especially, when *they are exercised towards us*, the affections, like a magnetized needle, tremble with life and turn towards their object.

2. The affections are not subject to the will;*

---

* We state the facts in the case, of which every man is conscious in his own experience, without regard to the theories of sects in religion or philosophy.

neither our own will nor any other will can directly control them. I can not will to love a being who does not appear to me lovely, and who does not exhibit the qualities adapted to move the affections; nor can I, by command, or by any other effort of will, cause another being to love me. The affections are not subject to command. You can not force another to love or respect, or even, from the heart, to obey. Such an attitude assumed to produce love would invariably produce disaffection rather than affection. No one (as a matter of fact) thinks the affections subject to the will, and, therefore, men never endeavor to obtain the affections of others solely by command, but by exhibiting such a character and conferring such favors as they know are adapted to move the heart. An effect could as easily exist without a cause as affection in the bosom of any human being which was not produced by goodness or excellencies seen, or believed to exist, in some other being.

3. The affections, although not governed by the will, do themselves greatly influence the will. All acts of will produced *entirely* by pure affection for another are disinterested. Cases of the affections influencing the will are common in the experience of every one. There is probably no one living who has not, at some period of his life, had affection for another, so that it gave more pleasure to please the object of his love than to please himself. *Love for another always influences the will to act in such a way as will please the object loved.* The individual loving acts in view of

the desires of the loved object, and such acts are *disinterested*, not being done with any selfish end in view, but for the sake of another. So soon as the affections move towards an object, the will is proportionably influenced to please and benefit that object; or, if a superior being, to obey his will and secure his favor.

4. All happy obedience must arise from affection. Affectionate obedience blesses the spirit which yields it, if the conscience approve the object loved and obeyed; while, on the contrary, no happiness can be experienced from obedience to any being that we do not love. To obey externally either God or a parent, from no other than interested motives, would be sin. The devil might be obeyed for the same reasons. Love must, therefore, constitute an essential element in all proper obedience to God.

5. When the affections of two beings are reciprocally fixed upon each other, they constitute a bond of union and sympathy peculiarly strong and tender; those things that affect the one affecting the other in proportion to the strength of affection existing between them. One conforms to the will of the other, not from a sense of obligation merely, but from choice; and the constitution of the soul is such that the sweetest enjoyment of which it is capable arises from the exercise of reciprocal affection.

6. When the circumstances of an individual are such that he is exposed to constant suffering and great danger, the more afflictive his situation the more grate-

ful love will he feel for affection and benefits received under such circumstances. If his circumstances were such that he could not relieve himself, and such that he must suffer greatly or perish, and, while in this condition, if another, moved by benevolent regard for him, should come to aid and save him, his affection for his deliverer would be increased by a sense of the danger from which he was rescued.

7. It is an admitted principle that protracted and close attention always fixes the fact attended to deeply in the memory; and the longer and more intensely the mind attends to any subject, other subjects proportionably lose their power to interest. The same is true in relation to the affections. The longer and more intensely we contemplate an object in that relation which is adapted to draw out the affections, the more deeply will the impression be made upon the heart, as well as upon the memory. The most favorable circumstances possible to fix an impression deeply upon the heart and memory are, first, that there should be protracted and earnest attention; and, second, that at the same time that the impression is made, the emotions of the soul should be alive with excitement. Without these, an impression made upon the heart and the memory would be slight and easily effaced; while, on the contrary, an impression made during intense attention and excited feeling will be engraved, as with a pen of steel, upon the tablets of the soul.

Now, with these principles in mind, mark the means used to fix the attention and to excite the susceptibilities of the Israelites, and, while in that state of attention and excitement, to draw their affections to God.

The children of Israel were suffering the most grievous bondage, which had arrived at almost an intolerable degree of cruelty and injustice. Just at this crisis the God of their fathers appears as their deliverer, and Moses is commissioned as his prophet. When the people are convened and their minds aroused by the hopes of deliverance, their attention is turned to two parties: one, Pharaoh, their oppressor and the slayer of their first-born; and the other the God of Abraham, who now appeared as their deliverer, espousing their cause and condescending personally to oppose himself to their oppressor. Then a scene ensues, adapted in all its circumstances to make a deep and enduring impression upon their memory and their heart. The God of Abraham seems, by his judgments, to have forced the oppressor to relent, and to let the people go. At this point hope and encouragement predominate in their minds. Now their oppressor's heart is hardened, and he renews his cruelty; but while their hopes are sinking, they are again revived and strengthened by finding that God continues to use means to induce Pharaoh to release the captives. Thus, for a considerable length of time, all the powers of excitability in their nature were aroused to activity. Towards that being who had so graciously interposed in their behalf they felt emotions of hope, gratitude, love, and admiration. Towards their oppressor feelings of an opposite character must have been engendered; and this state of excited suspense—the emotions vacillating between love and hatred, hope and fear—was continued until the impression became fixed deep in their souls.

Keeping in mind the fact that the more we need a benefactor and *feel* that need, the stronger will be our feelings of gratitude and love for the being who interposes in our behalf, notice further: When, through the interposition of the Almighty, the Israelites were delivered, and had advanced as far as the Red Sea, another appeal was made to their affections, which was most thrilling, and adapted to call, by one grand interposition, all their powers of gratitude and love into immediate and full exercise.

The army of the Israelites lay encamped on the margin of the Red Sea, when suddenly they were surprised by the approaching host of Pharaoh. Before them was the sea, and behind them an advancing hostile army. If they went forward, they would find death in the waves; if they returned backward, it would be to meet the swords of their pursuers. A rescue by earthly means from death, or bondage more severe than they had ever borne, was impossible. Just at this crisis of extremity Jehovah appears as their deliverer. The bosom of the pathless sea is cleft by the power of God. The stricken waters recoil upon themselves on either side. The Israelites pass over in safety. The Egyptian host enter and are overwhelmed in the waters.

Now it may be affirmed without qualification that, in view of the nature and circumstances of the Israelites, no combination of means, not including the self-sacrifice of the benefactor himself, could be so well adapted to elicit and absorb all the affections of the soul as this wonderful series of events. That this result was accomplished by these means is authenticated by the history given in the Bible. When the people were thus delivered they stood upon the other side of the sea, and their affections, in answer to the call which God had made upon them, gushed forth in thanksgiving and praise. Hear the response of their hearts, and their allusion to the cause which produced that response:

"O sing unto the LORD, for HE hath triumphed gloriously: the horse and his rider he hath thrown into the sea. The Lord is my strength and song, and he is become my SALVATION. He is my God; and I will prepare him a habitation; my father's God, and I will exalt him." (Ex. xv, 1, 2, etc.)

Thus was the attention of the whole nation turned to the true God. An impression of his goodness was fixed deeply in their memory, and their affections were drawn out and fastened upon the true object of worship. Now this, as was shown in the commencement of the chapter, was necessary, before they could offer worship either honorable or acceptable to God. The end was accomplished by means adapted to the nature of the human soul and to the circumstances of the Israelites; and by means which no being in the universe but the Maker of the soul could use. The demonstration is, therefore, perfect, that the Scripture narrative is true, and that no other narrative, differing materially from this in its principles could be true.

Chapter VI.

CONCERNING THE DESIGN AND NECESSITY OF THE MORAL LAW.

AT this stage of our progress it will be useful to recapitulate the conclusions at which we have arrived, and thus make a point of rest from which to extend our observation further into the plan of God for redeeming the world. This review is the more appropriate as we have arrived at a period in the history of God's providence with Israel, which presents them as a people prepared (so far as imperfect material could be prepared) to receive that model which God might desire to impress upon the nation.

1. They were bound to each other by all the ties of which human nature is susceptible, and thus rendered compact and united, so that every thing national, whether in sentiment or practice, would be received and cherished with unanimous and fervent and lasting attachment; and, furthermore, by a long and rigorous bondage they had been rendered, for the time being at least, humble and dependent. Thus they were disciplined by a course of providences, adapted to fit them to receive instruction from their benefactor with a teachable and grateful spirit.

2. Their minds were shaken off from idols; and Jehovah by a revelation made to them, setting forth

his name and nature, had revealed himself as a DIVINE BEING, and by his works had manifested his almighty power, so that when their minds were disabused of wrong views of the Godhead, an idea of the first true and essential nature of God was revealed to them, and they were thus prepared to receive a knowledge of the attributes of that divine essence.

3. They had been brought to contemplate God as their Protector and Savior. Appeals the most affecting and thrilling had been addressed to their affections; and they were thus attached to God as their almighty temporal Savior, by the ties of gratitude and love for the favor which he had manifested to them.

4. When they had arrived on the farther shore of the Red Sea, thus prepared to obey God and worship him with the heart, they were without laws either civil or moral. As yet they had never possessed any national or social organization. They were, therefore, prepared to receive, without predilection or prejudice, that system of moral instruction and civil polity which God might reveal as best adapted to promote the moral interests of the nation.

From these conclusions we may extend our vision forward into the system of revelation. This series of preparations would certainly lead the mind to the expectation that what was still wanting, and what they had been thus miraculously prepared to receive, would be granted, which was a knowledge of the moral character of God, and a moral law prescribing their duty to God and to men. Without this the plan that had been maturing for generations, and had been carried forward thus far by wonderful exhibitions of divine wisdom and power would be left unfinished just at the point where the finishing process was necessary.

But besides the strong probability which the previous preparation would produce that there would be a revelation of moral law, there are distinct and conclusive reasons evincing its necessity.

The whole experience of the world has confirmed the fact beyond the possibility of skepticism that man can not discover and establish a perfect rule of human duty. Whatever may be said of the many excellent maxims expressed by different individuals in different ages and nations, yet it is true that no *system* of duty to God and man, in any wise consistent with enlightened reason, has ever been established by human wisdom and sustained by !human sanctions, and, for reasons already stated,* such a fact never can occur.

But it may be supposed that each man has within himself sufficient light from reason, and sufficient admonition from conscience to guide himself, as an individual, in the path of truth and happiness. A single fact will correct such a supposition. Conscience, the great arbiter of the merit and demerit of human conduct has little intuitive sense of right, and is not guided entirely by reason, but is governed in a great measure by what men believe. Indeed, Faith is the legitimate regulator of the conscience. If a man has

---

* See chap. i, p. 34, et. seq.

correct views of duty to God and men, he will have a correct conscience; but if he can, by a wrong view of morals and of the character of God, be induced to believe that theft or murder, or any vice, is right, his conscience will be corrupted by his faith. When men are brought to believe, as they frequently do believe in heathen countries, that it is right to commit suicide or infanticide as a religious duty, their conscience condemns them if they do not perform the act. Thus that power in the soul which pronounces upon the moral character of human conduct, is itself dependent upon and regulated by the faith of the individual. It is apparent, therefore, that the reception and belief of a true rule of duty, accompanied with proper sanctions, will alone form in man a proper conscience. God has so constituted the soul that it is necessary, in order to the regulation of its moral powers, that it should have a rule of duty revealed under the sanction of its Maker's authority; otherwise its high moral powers would lie in dark and perpetual disorder.

Further, unless the human soul be an exception, God governs all things by laws adapted to their proper nature. The laws which govern the material world are sketched in the books on natural science; such are gravitation, affinity, mathematical motion. Those laws by which the irrational animal creation is controlled are usually called instincts. Their operation and design are sketched, to some extent, in treatises upon the instincts of animals. Such is the law which leads the beaver to build his dam, and all other animals to pursue some particular habits instead of others. All beavers, from the first one created to the present time, have been instinctively led to build a dam in the same manner, and so their instinct will lead them to build till the end of time. The law which drives them to the act is as necessitating as the law which causes the smoke to rise upwards. Nothing in the universe of God, animate or inanimate, is left without the government of appropriate law, unless that thing be the noblest creature of God—the human spirit. To suppose, therefore, that the human soul is thus left unguided by a revealed rule of conduct, is to suppose that God cares for the less and not the greater; to suppose that he would constitute the moral powers of the soul so that a law was necessary for their guidance, and then reveal none; to suppose, especially in the case of the Israelites, that he would prepare a people to receive and obey with a proper spirit this necessary rule of duty, and yet give no rule. But to suppose these things would be absurd; it follows, therefore, that God would reveal to the Israelites a law for the regulation of their conduct in morals and religion.

But physical law or necessitating instinct would not be adapted in its nature to the government of a rational and moral being. The application of either to the soul would destroy its free agency. God has made man intelligent, and thereby adapted his nature to a rule which he understands. Man has a will and a conscience; but he must understand the rule in order to will obedience, and he must believe the sanction by which the law is maintained before he can feel the obligation upon his conscience. A law, therefore, adapted to man's nature must be addressed to the understanding, sanctioned by suitable authority, and enforced by adequate penalties.

In accordance with these legitimate deductions, God gave the Israelites a rule of life—the Moral Law—succinctly comprehended in the Ten Commandments. And as affectionate obedience is the only proper obedience, he coupled the facts which were fitted to produce affection with the command to obey, saying, "I am Jehovah, thy God, which brought thee up out of the land of Egypt, and out of the house of bondage;" *therefore*, LOVE ME and KEEP MY COMMANDMENTS.*

---

* Deut. vi, *passim*.

Chapter VII.

CONCERNING THE DEVELOPMENT OF THE IDEA OF HOLINESS, AND ITS TRANSFER TO JEHOVAH AS AN ATTRIBUTE.

As yet the Israelites were little acquainted with any attribute of the I AM—Jehovah—except his infinite power and goodness; and his goodness was known to them only as manifested in kindness and mercy towards themselves as a peculiar people, distinguished from other nations, as the special objects of the divine favor. They had a disposition to worship Jehovah, and to regard the rights of each other according to his commandments; but they knew as yet little of his moral attributes. Of the attribute of holiness—purity from sin, and opposition of nature to all moral and physical defilement—they knew comparatively nothing. After the law had been given they knew that God required worship and obedience for himself, and just conduct towards others, but they did not know that his nature was hostile to all moral defilement of heart and life. And to this knowledge, as we have seen in the introduction, they could not of themselves attain.

At the period of the deliverance from Egypt every nation by which they were surrounded worshiped unholy beings. Now, how were the Jews to be extricated from this difficulty, and made to understand and feel the influence of the holy character of God? The Egyptian idolatry in which they had mingled was beastly and lustful; and one of their first acts of disobedience after their deliverance showed that their minds were still dark and their propensities corrupt. The golden calf which they desired should be erected for them was not designed as an act of apostasy from Jehovah, who had delivered them from Egyptian servitude. When the image was made, it was proclaimed to be that God which brought them up out of the land of Egypt; and when the proclamation of a feast, or idolatrous debauch, was issued by Aaron, it was denominated a feast, not to Isis or Osiris, but a feast to Jehovah, and as such they held it.* But they offered to the holy Jehovah the unholy worship of the idols of Egypt. Thus they manifested their ignorance of the holiness of his nature, as well as the corruption of their own hearts.

It was necessary, therefore, in order to promote right exercises of heart in religious worship, that the Israelites should be made acquainted with the holiness of God. The precise question, then, for solution is, How could the idea of God's holiness be conveyed to the minds of the Israelites? If it should be found that there is but one way in which it could be originated, according to the nature of mind, then it would follow, necessarily, that God would pursue that way, or he would have to alter the human constitution in order

---

*Ex. xxxii, 4, 5.

to communicate a knowledge of his attribute of holiness. But, as it is matter of fact that the constitution of the mind has not been altered, it follows that that method would be pursued which is in accordance with the nature of mind, to convey the necessary knowledge. Now all practical knowledge is conveyed to the understanding through the medium of the senses. Whatever may be said about innate ideas by speculative philosophers, still all agree that all acquired knowledge must reach the mind through the medium of one of the five senses, or upon the occasion of their exercise. Through the senses the knowledge of external objects is conveyed to the mind, and these simple ideas serve as material for reflection, comparison, and abstraction.

The etymology of the Hebrew language, as written by Moses and spoken by the Israelites, furnishes an interesting illustration of the origin of the few abstract terms with which their minds were familiar. The abstract ideas of the Hebrew tongue may even now, in most instances, be traced to the object or circumstance whence they originated. Thus the idea of power, among the Hebrews, was derived from the horn of an animal, and the same word in Hebrew which signifies horn likewise signifies power, and may be translated in either way to suit the sense. The idea was originally conveyed through the eye, by noticing that the strength of the animal was exerted through its horn. The force thus exerted, especially when the animal was enraged, was the greatest which fell under their observation, and, sometimes, in its effects it was disastrous and overwhelming. Hence the horn soon became a figure to denote power; and when the idea was once originated and defined in their minds they could apply it to any object which produced a strong effect either upon the bodies or the minds of men. An idea of power likewise originated from the human hand, because through it man exerted his strength. The same word in Hebrew still expresses both the object and the idea derived from it. "Life and death are in the power of the tongue," reads literally, "Life and death are in the *hand* of the tongue." Sunshine in Hebrew is synonymous with happiness, the idea being originated by experiencing the pleasant feelings produced by the effects of a sunny day; and when thus originated it was applied to the same and similar feelings produced by other causes. The abstract idea of judgment or justice is derived from a word which signifies to *cut* or *divide*, it being originated by the circumstance that when the primitive hunters had killed a stag or other prey, one divided the flesh with a knife among those who assisted in the pursuit, distributing a just portion to each. Thus the act of cutting and dividing their prey, which was the first circumstance that called into exercise and placed before their senses the principle of justice, was the circumstance from which they derived this most important abstract idea.

Other instances might be mentioned. These are sufficient to show the manner in which the abstract ideas of the Hebrews were originated. And so every new idea which found a place in their understanding had to be originated, primarily, by an impression made by external objects upon the senses.

Further, all ideas which admit of the signification of more or most perfect can be originated only by a comparison of one object with another. More lovely, or more pure, can only be predicated of one thing by comparison with another which it excels in one of these respects. By a series of comparisons, each one exceeding the last in beauty or purity, an idea of the highest degree of perfection may be produced. Thus one flower may be called lovely, another more lovely, and the rose the most lovely; and the idea of the *superior* beauty of the rose would be originated by the comparison or contrast between it and other flowers of less beauty. It is not said that the rose would not appear lovely without comparison, but the idea of its *superior* loveliness is originated by comparison, and it could be derived in no other way.

With these principles in mind we return to the inquiry, *How could the idea of God's holiness or moral purity be conveyed to the minds of the Jews?*

First, mark the principles. (1.) There was not an object in the material world which would convey to the mind the idea of God's holiness. (2.) The idea, therefore, would have to be originated, and thrown into their mind, through the senses, by a process instituted for that express purpose. (3.) The plan to originate the idea in order to meet the constitution of the mind, must consist of a series of comparisons.

Now, mark the correspondency between these principles, founded upon the laws of the mind, and that system devised to instruct the Israelites in the knowledge of God.

In the outset, the animals common to Palestine were divided by command of Jehovah into clean and unclean; in this way a distinction was made, and the one class in comparison with the other was deemed to be of a purer and better kind. From the class thus distinguished as more pure than the other, one was selected to offer as a sacrifice. It was not only to be chosen from the clean beasts, but as an individual it was to be without spot or blemish. Thus it was in their eyes purer than the other class, and purer than other individuals of its own class. This sacrifice the people were not deemed worthy in their own persons to offer unto Jehovah, but it was to be offered by a class of men who were distinguished from their brethren, purified and set apart for the service of the priest's office. Thus the idea of purity originated from two sources; the purified priest and the pure animal *purified* were united in the offering of the sacrifice. But before the sacrifice could be offered it was washed with clean water, and the priest had, in some cases, to wash himself and officiate without his sandals. Thus when one process of comparison after another had attached the idea of superlative purity to the sacrifice in offering it to Jehovah, in order that the contrast between the purity of God and the highest degrees of earthly purity might be seen, neither priest, people, nor sacrifice was deemed sufficiently pure to come into his presence, but the offering was made in the court without the holy of holies. In this manner, by a process of comparison, the character of God in point of purity was placed indefinitely above themselves and their sacrifices.*

And not only in the sacrifices, but throughout the whole Levitical economy, the idea of purity pervaded all its ceremonies and observances. The camp was purified, the people were purified; every thing was purified and re-purified, and each process of the ordinances was designed to reflect purity upon the others, until finally that idea of purity formed in the mind and rendered intense by the convergence of so many rays, was by comparison referred to the idea of God, and the idea of God in their minds being that of an infinitely powerful and good Spirit, hence, purity as a characteristic or attribute of such a nature would necessarily assume a moral aspect; because it appertained

---

* It is not argued that no other end was designed and accomplished by the arbitrary separation of animals into classes of clean and unclean. By this means the Jews were undoubtedly excluded from partaking in the feasts of the heathen around, who ate those animals which were forbidden to them. An excellent writer observes that it is characteristic of the wisdom of God to accomplish many ends by a single act of providence.

to a moral being, it would become *moral purity, or holiness*. Thus they learned in the sentiment of Scripture that God was of too *pure* eyes to look upon iniquity.

That the idea of moral purity in the minds of the Israelites was thus originated by the machinery of the Levitical dispensation, is supported, not only by the philosophy of the thing, but by many allusions in the Scriptures. Such allusions are frequent both in the writers of the old and of the new dispensations; evidencing that, in their minds, the idea of moral purity was still symbolized by physical purity. The rite of baptism is founded upon this symbolical analogy, the external washing with water being significant of the purifying influence of the Holy Spirit. St. John saw in vision the undefiled in heart clothed with linen pure and white; evincing that, to the mind of the Jew, such vestments as the high-priest wore when he entered the holy of holies were still emblematical of moral purity. In the Epistle to Hebrews, which is an apostolic exposition of the spiritual import of the Levitical institution, so far as that institution particularly concerns believers under the New Testament dispensation, we have the foregoing view of the design of ceremonial purification expressly confirmed. "It was, therefore, necessary," says Paul to the Hebrews, "that the patterns of things in the heavens should be purified with these [*i. e.* with these purifying processes addressed to the senses], but the heavenly things themselves with better sacrifices than these;" the plain instruction of which is, that the parts and processes of the Levitical economy were patterns addressed to the senses of unseen things in heaven, and that the purifying of those patterns indicated the spiritual purity of the spiritual things which they represented.

There is, finally, demonstrative evidence of the fact, that the idea of perfect moral purity as connected with the idea of God is *now*, and always *has been*, the same which was originated and conveyed to the minds of the Jews by the machinery of the Levitical dispensation. The Hebrew word קדש— *quadhosh*—was used to express the idea of purity as originated by the tabernacle service. The literal definition is, *pure, to be pure, to be purified for sacred uses.* The word thus originated and conveying this meaning is employed in the Scriptures to express the moral purity or holiness of God.*
In the New Testament this word is translated by the Greek term ἅγιος, *hagios*, but the Hebrew idea is connected with the Greek word. In King James's version this Greek word is rendered by the Saxon term *holy*, the Saxon word losing its original import (*whole, wholly*), and taking that of the Hebrew derived through the Greek. So that our idea of the holiness of God is the same which was originated by the Levitical ceremonies; and there is no other word, so far as I have been able to examine, in any language which conveys

---

* שם קדשי—my holy name. Lev. xx, 3.

this idea; nor is there any idea among any people that approximates closely to the Scripture idea of holiness, unless the words received some shades of its signification from the Bible.*

Here, then, the idea of God's moral purity was conveyed by the Mosaic economy in a manner in accordance with the constitution and the condition of the Jewish mind. This same idea has descended from the Hebrew, through the Greek, to our own language; and there is, so far as known, no other word in the world which conveys to the mind the true idea of God's moral purity, but that originated by the institution which God prescribed to Moses upon the mount.†

The demonstration then is conclusive, both from philosophy and fact, that the true and necessary idea of God's attribute of holiness was originated by the

---

* One of the principal difficulties which the missionary meets with, according to letters in the missionary reports, is that of conveying to the mind of the heathen the idea of the holiness of God. They find no such idea in their minds, and they can use no words in their language by which to convey the full and true force of the thought. The true idea, therefore, if communicated at all, must be conveyed by a periphrasis, and by labored illustration. This obstacle will be one of the most difficult to surmount in all languages, and it can not be perfectly overcome till the Christian teacher becomes perfectly familiar with the language of those whom he wishes to instruct.

† Ex. xxv, 9.

"patterns" of the Levitical economy, and that it could have been communicated to mankind, at the first, in no other way.*

---

* The foundation principle of that school of skepticism, at the head of which are the atheistical materialists, is that all knowledge is derived through the medium of the senses, and that as God is not an object of sense, men can have no knowledge of his being or attributes. Now these deductions show that the truth of revealed religion may be firmly established upon their own proposition.

Chapter VIII.

CONCERNING THE ORIGIN OF THE IDEAS OF JUSTICE AND MERCY, AND THEIR TRANSFER TO THE CHARACTER OF JEHOVAH.

HOLINESS and justice, although they convey to the mind ideas somewhat distinct from each other, yet the import of the one is shaded into that of the other. Holiness signifies the purity of the divine nature from moral defilement, while justice signifies the relation which holiness causes God to sustain to men as the subjects of the divine government. In relation to God one is subjective, declaring his freedom from sin; the other objective, declaring his opposition to sin as the transgression of the divine law. The Israelites might know that God was holy, and that he required of them clean hands and a clean heart in worship, and yet not understand the full demerit of transgressing the will of God or the intensity of the divine opposition to sin. God had given them the moral law, and they knew that he required them to obey it; but what in the mind of God was the proper desert of disobeying it, they did not know. They had been accustomed, like all idolators, to consider the desert of moral transgression uncertain and unequal. Now they had to learn the immutable justice of the Supreme Being, that his holiness was not a passive quality, but an active attribute of his nature, and not only the opposite, but the antagonist principle to sin.

In what manner, then, could a knowledge of the Divine Justice, or of the demerit of sin in the sight of God, be conveyed to the minds of the Jews?

There is but one way in which any being can manifest to other minds the opposition of his nature to sin. A lawgiver can manifest his views of the demerit of transgression in no other way than by the *penalty* which he inflicts upon the transgressor. In all beings who have authority to make law for the obedience of others, the conscience is the standard which regulates the amount of punishment that should be inflicted upon the disobedient. And the measure of punishment which conscience dictates is just in proportion to the opposition which the lawgiver feels to the transgression of his law; *i. e.*, the amount of regard which he has for his own law will graduate the amount of opposition which he will feel to its transgression. The amount of opposition which any being feels to sin is in proportion to the holiness of that being, and conscience will sanction penalty up to the amount of opposition which he feels to crime.

If the father of a family felt no regard for the law of the Sabbath, his conscience would not allow him to punish his children for violating, by folly or labor, a law which he did not himself respect. But a father who felt a sacred regard for the divine law would be required by his conscience to cause his children to respect the Sabbath, and to punish them if they disobeyed. The penalty which one felt to be wrong the other would feel to be right, because the disposition of the one towards the law was different from the other.

The principle, then, is manifest, that the more holy and just any being is, the more he is opposed to sin, and the higher penalty will his conscience sanction as the desert of transgressing the divine law. Now God being infinitely holy, he is therefore infinitely opposed to sin, and the divine conscience will enforce penalty accordingly.

This is the foundation of penalty in the divine mind. The particular point of inquiry is, *How could the desert of sin, as it existed in the mind of God, be revealed to the Israelites?*

If the penalty inflicted is sanctioned by the conscience of the lawgiver, it follows, as has been shown, that the opposition of his nature to the crime is in exact proportion to the penalty which he inflicts upon the criminal. Penalty, therefore, inflicted upon the transgressor, is the only way by which the standard of justice as it exists in the mind of God could be revealed to men.

The truth of this principle may be made apparent by illustration. Suppose a father were to express his will in relation to the government of his family, and the regulations were no sooner made than some of his children should resist his authority and disobey his commands. Now, suppose the father should not punish the offenders, but treat them as he did his obedient children. By so doing he would encourage the disobedient, discourage the obedient, destroy his own authority, and make the impression upon the minds of all his children that he had no regard for the regulations which he had himself made. And, further, if these regulations were for the general good of the family, by not maintaining them he would convince the obedient that he did not regard their best interests, but was the friend of the rebellious. And if he were to punish for the transgression but lightly, they would suppose that he estimated but lightly a breach of his commands; and they could not, from the constitution of their minds, suppose otherwise. But if the father, when one of the children transgressed, should punish him and exclude him from favor till he submitted to his authority and acknowledged with a penitent spirit his offense, then the household would be convinced that the father's will was imperative, and that the only alternative presented to them was affectionate submission or exclusion from the society of their father and his obedient children. Thus the amount of the father's regard for his law, his interest in the well-being of his obedient children and the opposition of his nature to disobedience, would be graduated in every child's mind by the penalty which he inflicted for the transgression of his commands.

So in the case of an absolute lawgiver: his hostility to crime could be known only by the penalty which he inflicted upon the criminal. If for the crime of theft he were to punish the offender only by the imposition of a trifling fine, the impression would be made upon every mind that he did not at heart feel much hostility to the crime of larceny. If he had the power and did not punish crime at all, he would thus reveal to the whole nation that he was in league with criminals, and himself a criminal at heart.

So in relation to murder: if he were to let the culprit go free or inflict upon him but a slight penalty, he would thus show that his heart was tainted with guilt, and that there was no safety for good men under his government. But should he fix a penalty to transgression, declare it to all his subjects, and visit every criminal with punishment in proportion to his guilt, he would show to the world that he regarded the law, and was opposed directly and forever to its transgression.

In like manner and in no other way could God manifest to men his infinite justice and his regard for the laws of his kingdom. Did he punish for sin with but a slight penalty, the whole universe of mind would have good reason to believe that the God of heaven was but little opposed to sin. Did he punish it with the highest degree of penalty, it would be evidence to the universe that his nature was in the highest degree opposed to sin and attached to holiness.

Now, whatever may be said in relation to the application of these principles to future rewards and punishments, one thing will be apparent to all, which is all that the present argument requires to be admitted; that is, the mind of man would receive an idea of the amount of God's opposition to sin only by the amount of penalty which he inflicted upon the sinner.

Having ascertained these premises, we return to the inquiry, *How could the demerit of sin in the sight of God or the idea of God's attribute of justice be conveyed to the minds of the Jews?*

The people had now in a good degree a knowledge of what sin was. In addition to the light of natural conscience which might guide them to some extent in relation to their duties to each other, they had the moral law, with the commentary of Moses defining its precepts, and applying them to the conduct of life. Their minds were thus enlightened in relation to sin in the following particulars: First, those acts which were a transgression of the positive precepts of the law; second, omissions of duties enjoined in the law; and, third, many acts which the spirit of the law would condemn, but which might not be defined in any particular precept, would now be noticed by enlightened conscience, as sin against Jehovah, their holy benefactor and the giver of the law.

Having thus been taught what was sin of commission and omission, one obvious design of the institution of sacrifices,* and one which has been perceived

---

*The question whether the sacrifices, and the particular regulations concerning them, were of divine origin, does not affect the argument. Whether they were originally instituted by divine command, or whether Moses, acting under divine guidance, modified an existing institution and adapted it to the divine purposes, both the design and the end accomplished would be the same. There are good reasons, however, for the opinion that **sacrifices for sin** were of divine appointment.

and understood, both by the Jews and Gentiles, was to convey to the mind the just demerit and proper penalty of sin.

There were three classes of sacrifices in the old dispensation in which death was inflicted. The first, which Gentiles as well as Jews were permitted to offer, was the holocaust, or whole burnt-offering, which was entirely consumed by fire. Sacrifices of this description seem to have been offered from the earliest ages. They were offered, as the best informed think, as an acknowledgment of and atonement for general sinfulness of life. They seem to have had reference to the fact, of which every man is conscious, that he often violates known duty and does many things which the light of nature and conscience teaches him not to do.

After the whole burnt-offering was the sin-offering, sacrificed for an atonement, when the individual had transgressed any specific precept of the moral law.

The trespass-offering differed only from the sin-offering, as the learned suppose, in this, that it was a sacrifice for sins of omission, or for the non-performance of duty, while the sin-offering was made for a violation of the specific precepts of the Moral Law. Whether the design of the different classes of sacrifices was as above specified or not, is not material, further than it shows how nicely the forms of the Levitical economy were adjusted to meet that varied consciousness of sin which the precepts of the law and an enlightened conscience would produce in the human soul. The material point to which attention is necessary, with reference to the present discussion, is that by which the death and destruction of the animal offered in sacrifice was made to represent the desert of the sinner.

When an individual brought a sacrifice he delivered it to the priest to be slain. He then laid his hands upon its head, thereby, in a form well understood among the Jews, transferring to it his sins; and then the life of the sacrifice was taken as a substitute for his own life. He was thus taught that the transgression of the law, or any act of sin against God, was worthy of death, and that the sacrifice suffered that penalty in his stead.

Further, the Jews had been taught that the blood of the sacrifice was its life; or, rather, the principle upon which the life of the body depended. Upon this subject they had the following express instruction: "For the life of the flesh is the blood; and I have given it to you upon the altar to make an atonement for your souls; for it is the blood that maketh an atonement for the soul."* Now this blood, which the Jews were thus taught to believe was the life of the sacrifice, was repeatedly sprinkled by the priest upon the mercy-seat and towards the holy place, thus presenting the life of the sacrifice immediately in the presence of God (the ineffable light, or symbol of God's presence, rested over the mercy-seat between the cherubim), signifying, as plainly as forms and shadows and external types could signify, that life had been rendered up to God to make an atonement for their souls.

---

* Lev. xvii, 11.

Thus the idea was conveyed to their mind through the senses that the desert of sin in the sight of God was the death of the soul. And while they stood praying in the outer court of the tabernacle, and beheld the dark volume of smoke ascending from the fire that consumed the sacrifice which was *burning in their stead*, how awful must have been the impression of the desert of sin made by that dark volume of ascending smoke! The idea was distinct and deeply impressed, that God's justice was a consuming fire to sinners, and that their souls escaped only through a vicarious atonement.

As a picture in a child's primer will convey an idea to the infant mind long before it can be taught by abstract signs, so the Jews, in the infancy of their knowledge of God, and before there were any abstract signs to convey that knowledge, had thrown into their minds through the senses the two essential ideas of God's justice and mercy—his justice, in that the wages of sin is the death of the soul; and his mercy, in that God would pardon the sinner if he confessed his sin, acknowledged the life of his soul forfeited, and offered the life of the sacrifice as his substitute.

In this manner an idea of the desert of sin was conveyed to the minds of the Jews, God's law honored, and the utter hostility of the lawgiver to sin clearly manifested; and God's mercy was likewise revealed as stated in the preceding paragraph. Thus in a manner accordant with the circumstances of the Jews, and by means adapted in their operation to the constitution of nature, was the knowledge of God's attribute of Justice, and the relation which Mercy sustains to that attribute, fully revealed in the world; and in view of the nature of things it could have been revealed in no other way.*

---

* Inquiring readers of the Old Testament often find many things announced in the name of God which must seem to them inconsistent with the majesty of the divine nature, unless they view those requirements in the light of the inquiry, "What impressions were they adapted to make upon the Jewish mind?" There are but few readers of the Old Testament who read on this subject intelligently. In this remark we do not refer to the historical or preceptive portions of these writings, but to the elements of the Mosaic institution. In order to see the design of many items of the system, we must consider those items as exhibitions to the senses, designed chiefly, perhaps only, to produce right ideas, or to correct erroneous ones then existing in the minds of the Jews. The inquiry ought not to be, What impression are they adapted to produce upon our minds concerning God? but, What impression would the particular revelation make upon THEIR minds? An instance or two will illustrate these remarks.

The adaptation to accomplish a necessary end is apparent in the scene at Sinai. The Israelites had been accustomed to an idolatry where the most common familiarities were practiced with the idol gods. The idea of reverence and majesty which belongs to the character of God had been lost by attaching the idea of divinity to the objects of sense. It was necessary, therefore, that the idea of God should now be clothed in their minds with that reverence and majesty which properly belongs to it. The scene at Sinai was adapted to produce, and did produce for the time being, the right impression. The mountain was made to tremble to its base. A cloud of darkness covered its summit, from which the lightnings leaped out and thunders uttered their voices. In the words of a New Testament writer, there was "darkness, and blackness, and tempest." It was ordered that neither man nor beast should touch the mountain, lest they should be visited with death. The exhibition in all its forms was adapted to produce that sense of majesty and awe in view of the divine character which the Israelites needed to feel. To minds subjected to the influence of other circumstances than those which affected the character of the Israelites in Egypt, such manifestations might not be necessary; but in the case of the Jews, accustomed as they had been to witness a besotting familiarity with idols, these manifestations were directly adapted to counteract low views of the divine character, and to inspire the soul with suitable reverence in view of the infinite majesty and eternal power of the being with whom they had to do.

The testimony of the Bible in relation to the design of the exhibition at Sinai corroborates the views that have been given. "When the people saw it, they removed and stood afar off, and they said unto Moses, Speak thou unto us and we will hear: but let not God speak unto us lest we die. And Moses said unto the people, Fear not, for God has come to prove you, and that his fear may be before your faces that ye sin not." (Ex. xx, 18, 19.)

The scene which occurred afterwards evinced the necessity of this exhibition, and developed the result of the proof (trial) that was made of their character. In the absence of Moses they required an image of Jehovah to be made, and they feasted and "played"—this last word having a licentious import—in its presence. Thus, after trial of the strongest exhibitions upon their mind, some of them proved themselves so incorrigibly attached to licentious idolatry that they desired to worship Jehovah under the character of the Egyptian calf. They thus proved themselves unfit material, too corrupt for the end in view, and they were, in accordance with the reason of the case, destroyed.

Another conviction necessary to be lodged in the minds of the Israelites, and impressed deeply and frequently upon their hearts, was faith in the present and overruling God. This was the more necessary as no visible image of Jehovah was allowed in the camp. There were but two methods possible by which their minds could be convinced of the immediate presence and power of God controlling all the events of their history. Either such exhibitions must be made that they would see certain ends accomplished without human instrumentality, or they must see human instrumentality clothed with a power which it is not possible in the nature of things it should in itself possess. The circumstances connected with the fall of Jericho will illustrate the case. The people were required to surround the city, by a silent procession during seven days, bearing the sacred ark, and blowing with rude instruments which they used for trumpets. On the seventh day the people were to shout after they had compassed the city seven times; and when they shouted, according to a divine promise, the walls of the city fell to the ground. Now, here was a process of means in which there was no adaptation to produce the external effect, in order that the INTERNAL effect, the great end of all revelation, might be produced; that they might be taught to recognize Jehovah as the present God of nature and providence, and rest their faith on him.

If the Israelites had, in this case, used the common instrumentalities to secure success; if they had destroyed the wall with instruments of war, or scaled its height with ladders, and thus overcome by the strength of their own arm, or the aid of their own devices, instead of being led to humble reliance upon God, and to recognize his agency in their behalf, they would have seen in the means which they had used a cause adequate to produce the effect, and they would have forgotten the First Cause, upon whose power they were dependent. Second causes were avoided, in order that they might see the connection between the First Cause and the effect produced; human instrumentality stood in abeyance, in order that the divine agency might be recognized. Thus they were taught to have faith in God, and to rely upon the presence and the power of the invisible Jehovah.

Chapter IX.

CONCERNING THE TRANSITION FROM THE MATERIAL SYSTEM, BY WHICH RELIGIOUS IDEAS WERE CONVEYED THROUGH THE SENSES, TO THE SPIRITUAL SYSTEM, IN WHICH ABSTRACT IDEAS WERE CONVEYED BY WORDS AND PARABLES.

HUMAN language has always advanced from its first stage, in which ideas are acquired directly through the medium of the senses, to the higher state, in which abtsract ideas are conveyed by appropriate words and signs. When an idea is once formed by outward objects, and a word formed representing that idea, it is then no longer necessary or desirable that the object which first originated the idea should longer be associated in the mind with the idea itself. It is even true that the import of abstract ideas suffers from a co-existence in the mind of the abstract thought with the idea of the object which originated it. Thus the word spirit now conveys a distinct idea to the mind of pure spiritual existence; but the distinctness and power of the idea is impaired by remembering that the word from which it was derived originally signified wind, and that the word itself was originated in the first place by the wind. So in other cases: although the ideas of abstract and spiritual things can be originated, primarily, only from outward objects, yet when they have been originated, and the spiritual idea connected with the sign or word conveying its proper sense, it is desirable, in order to their greatest force and perspicuity, that their connection with materiality should be broken off in the mind.

In all written languages this advancement from one stage of perfection to another, by the addition of abstract ideas, can be traced; and experience teaches, incontrovertibly, that the advancement of human language, as above described, and the advancement of human society, are dependent upon each other.

The preceding principles being applied to the subject under consideration, it would follow that the Mosaic machinery, which formed the abstract ideas conveying the knowledge of God's true character, would no longer be useful after those ideas were originated, defined, and connected with the words which expressed their abstract or spiritual import. It would follow, therefore, that the machinery would be entirely dispensed with whenever it had answered the entire design for which it was put into operation. Whenever the Jews were cured of idolatry, and had obtained true ideas of the attributes of the true God, then the dispensation of shadows and ceremonies, which "could not make the comers thereunto perfect," would, according to the reason of things, pass away, and give place to a more perfect and more spiritual dispensation.

We find, accordingly, that the machinery of the tabernacle was gradually removed, it never having existed in perfection after the location of the tribes in Palestine. They sojourned in the wilderness until those who had come out of Egypt died. The generation who succeeded them had the advantage of having received their entire education through the medium of the Mosaic institution, and thus of being freed from vicious habits and remembrances contracted in idolatrous society.

Afterwards the prophets held an intermediate place between the material dispensation of Moses and the pure spirituality of that of Christ. In the prophetic books, especially the later ones, there is an evident departure from a reliance upon the external forms, and an application of the ideas connected with those forms to internal states of mind. Their views of the old dispensation were more spiritual than the views of those who lived near the origin of the institution. And in the dispensation of the Messiah, the prophets evidently expected clearer light and purer spirituality.

The state of the case, then, is this: The old dispensation was necessary and indispensable in itself and in its place, but it was neither designed nor adapted to continue; the knowledge of divine things which it generated was necessary for all men, but as yet it was circumscribed to a small portion of the human family: the point of inquiry now presents itself, *How could this essential knowledge concerning the Divine Nature and attributes be extended throughout the world?*

There would be but two methods possible: either the same processes and the same cumbrous machinery (which were a "burden" that an apostle affirmed neither he nor his fathers were able to bear) must be established in every nation and kindred and tribe of the human family, and thus each nation be disciplined and educated by itself, or one nation must be prepared and disciplined, their propensity to idolatry destroyed, the ideas coined in the die prepared by Jehovah thrown into their minds, and then, being thus prepared, they might be made the instruments of transferring those ideas into the languages of other nations.* If the Almighty were to adopt the first method, it would exclude men from benevolent labor for the spiritual good of each other; and, besides, the history of the process with the Jews, as well as the reason of the thing, would indicate that the latter

---

*There is a common and, to some minds, a weighty objection against the truth of revealed religion, stated as follows: If God ever gave a religion to the world, why did he not reveal it to all men, and reveal it at once and perfectly, so that no one could doubt? If this had been possible, it might not have been expedient; but the nature of things, as we have seen, rendered it impossible to give man a revelation in such a manner.

method would be the one which the Maker would adopt.

But in order to the diffusion of the knowledge of God by the latter method, some things would be necessary as prerequisites, among which are the following:

1. That the Jews, who possessed these ideas, should be scattered throughout the world, and that they should be thus scattered long enough before the time of the general diffusion of divine knowledge to have become familiar with the languages of the different nations where they sojourned. This would be necessary in order that, by speaking in other tongues, they might transfer into them their own ideas of divine things, by attaching those ideas to words in the respective languages which they spoke, or by introducing into those languagas words and phrases of Hebrew origin, conveying the revealed ideas. Whether the different languages were acquired by miraculous or by human instrumentality, there would be no other way possible of transferring ideas from one language to another but by the methods above mentioned.

2. It would be necessary, before the Jews were thus scattered, that their propensity to idolatry should be entirely subdued; otherwise they would, as they had frequently done before, fall into the abominable habits of the nations among whom they were dispersed.*

---

* Idolatry is one of the most unconquerable of all the corrupt propensities of the human soul. Miracles under the new dispensation had scarcely ceased, the apostolic

3. The new and spiritual system should be first propagated among those who understood both the spiritual import of the Hebrew language, and likewise the language of the other nations to whom the Gospel was to be preached. It was necessary that the new dispensation should be committed first to the Jews, who were scattered in the surrounding nations, because, as we have seen, they were the only individuals immediately prepared to communicate it to others.

Now, the following facts are matters of authentic history:

1. By instruction and discipline the Jews were entirely cured of the propensity to idolatry; so much so that their souls abhorred idols.

2. They were, and had been for many generations, dispersed among all nations of the Roman world; but still in their dispersion they retained their peculiar ideas, and multitudes of this peculiar people assembled out of all countries, at least once a year, at the city of Jerusalem, to worship Jehovah; and it was while the multitude were thus assembled that the Gospel was first preached to them; and preached, as was proper it should be, by power and miracle, in order that those present might know assuredly that the dispensation was from Heaven.

---

fathers were scarcely cold in their graves, before idolatrous forms were again superinduced upon the pure spirituality of the holy Gospel, and in the Papal Church the curse continues till this hour.

3. The new dispensation was likewise introduced, in the first place, among the Jews who continued to reside in Palestine, and when a sufficient number of them were fully initiated, persecutions were caused to arise, which scattered them abroad among the nations; and the Gentile languages not being known to them, they were miraculously endowed with the gift of tongues, that they might communicate to others the treasures of divine knowledge committed to them.

Thus when the old dispensation had fulfilled its design in disciplining the Jews, in imparting first ideas, and thus, as a "schoolmaster," preparing the people for the higher instruction of Christ, and when the fullness of the times had come, that the means and the material were prepared to propagate the spiritual truth of the new dispensation, then the Mosaic cycle would appropriately close; it would not be consistent that it should remain longer, for the plain reason given by Jesus himself, that new wine should not be put into old bottles, nor the old and imperfect forms be incorporated with the new and spiritual system.

Therefore it was, that so soon as the new dispensation had been introduced, and its foundations firmly laid, Jerusalem, the center of the old economy, with the temple and all things pertaining to the ritual service, was at once and completely destroyed, and the old system vanished away forever. It would not have been expedient for God to destroy the old system sooner, because it was necessary to engraft the new system upon the old; and it ought not to have remained longer, for the reasons above stated.*

---

* It was necessary that the old system should be destroyed at this time, in order to throw the Jews upon Christ, as the sacrifice for their sins. Under the old dispensation the sacrifices for sin were allowed to continue to the end. From this sacrifice they were taught to hope for pardon. An idea had been, by the process which God himself instituted, originated in their mind, that death must ensue for sin; but by transferring their sins to be the head of the sacrifice, it died as a vicarious expiation, and they lived. It had become a part, almost, of the Jewish mind, that they could not hope for pardon unless the sacrifice was offered. They felt that their life was forfeited by sin, and they were unpardoned until the sacrifice was made, and it could be made nowhere else but at Jerusalem. Now, God destroyed Jerusalem, and caused the offering for sin to cease, and entirely annihilated the possibility of their ever again expiating their sins by the bloody sacrifices; they were, therefore, shut up to the doctrine of Christ's sacrifice for sin. By the destruction of Jerusalem the alternative was presented to the Jews: Accept of Christ's sacrifice, or you have no propitiation for your sins.

Chapter X.

CONCERNING THE MEDIUM OF CONVEYING TO MEN PERFECT INSTRUCTION IN DOCTRINE AND DUTY.

THE knowledge which the old dispensation was designed to generate had been transmitted into the minds of the Jews; and the Jews had been prepared to transmit the abstract import of those spiritual ideas into other languages. The Mosaic institution, having accomplished its design, was about to "vanish away" and give place to the new dispensation, which would end the series of God's revealed instructions by giving men a perfect system of religion, accompanied by those aids and influences which would be adapted to develop and perfect man's moral powers, and render him, in his present condition, as perfect as his nature and his circumstances would allow.

At this point of our progress the inquiry presents itself, *What can we learn, from the present constitution of things, concerning the medium or instrumentality that God would adopt in giving mankind a perfect system of religion?*

When the ideas that conveyed the knowledge of God were understood by the people, human language would then become the proper medium of communication. The very fact that the ideas were generated and thrown into language evinces that language was designed, eventually, to be the medium through which they should be transmitted to the world. When the ideas were prepared, as has been stated, then all that would be necessary, in order to the further and more perfect communication of knowledge, would be, that men should have a teacher to use this language, to expand, illustrate, and apply these ideas; and by these give definitions, and illustrate and spiritualize other ideas when necessary.

Further, man's senses are constituted with an adaptation to the external world, and his intellectual constitution is adapted to intercourse with his fellow-man. The delicate bony structure of the ear, which conveys sounds from the tympanum to the sensorium, is nicely adjusted by the Maker to appreciate and convey the tones and modulations of the human voice. Human gesture, likewise, and the expression of the countenance and the eye, are auxiliary to human language in conveying instruction. The nature of man, therefore, is adapted, both physically and intellectually, to receive knowledge by communications from one of his own species. If God designed that an angel should instruct the human family, one of two things would have to be done: either the human constitution would have to be elevated and adapted to intercourse with a being of a higher order in the scale of creation, or that being would have to let down his nature to human capacity, and thus adapt himself to intercourse with human natures. And it would even be requisite that the teacher should not assume the highest condition of humanity in order that his instructions should accomplish the greatest general good; nor should his communications be made in the most cultivated and elevated style of language. If he would instruct the common mind in the best manner, he must use common language and common illustrations; and if God (blessed be his name!) were himself to instruct human nature, *as it is*, the same means would be necessary.

Another step: Man is so constituted that he learns by example better than by precept. Theory without practice, or precept without example, does not constitute a perfect system of instruction. The theory of surveying, however perfectly it may be taught in college, never makes a practical surveyor. An artist may give a most perfect theory of his art to his apprentices or those whom he wishes to instruct in a knowledge of his business, but if he would have them become practical artists themselves, he must, with tools in hand, practice his own instructions before the eyes of the learner. In the language of the trades, he must "show how it's done." Such, then, is the nature of man, that in order to a perfect system of instruction, there must be both precept and practice.

Now, there can be but one perfect model of human nature; and man could not be removed to some other planet, nor out of his present circumstances, to be instructed. If the Almighty, therefore, designed ever to give a perfect and final system of instruction to mankind, it could be done only by placing in this world a perfect human nature—a being who would not only give perfect precepts, but who would practice those precepts before the eyes of men. If such a being were placed among men, who, amid all the perplexities, difficulties, and trials which affect men in their present condition, would exhibit perfect action of body, heart, and mind in all his relations of life, and in all his duties to God and man, that would be a model character, practicing the precepts of the divine law in man's present circumstances. The example of an angel, or of any being of a different order from man, would be of no benefit to the human family. Man must see his duties, as man, exemplified in his own nature. *Human nature could be perfected only by following a perfect model of human nature.* But with the rule of duty in his hand, and a model character before him, man would have a system of instruction perfectly adapted to his *nature*, and adapted to *perfect* his nature. If God, therefore, designed to give man a final and perfect system of instruction, he would adopt the method thus adapted to the constitution which he has given his creatures.

Now, JESUS CHRIST IS THAT MODEL CHARACTER. He assumed human nature; came to the earth, man's residence; expounded and illustrated the law in human language; gave it its spiritual import, and applied it to the different circumstances and conditions of human life. He removed the false glosses which the ignorance and the prejudices of men had attached to it;

he modified or rescinded those permissions or clauses which were accommodated to the darkness of former times and the imperfections of the Jewish system, and then, by applications the most striking and definite, he showed the bearing of the rule of duty upon all varieties of human action.

And, further, the law being thus defined and applied, in order that the world might have a model character, he conformed himself to all its requirements; and in order that that model might be a guide in all the varied circumstances in which some of the family of man might be placed, Jesus placed himself in all those circumstances, and *acted* in them. Is man surrounded by a sinful and suffering world? So was Jesus. Does he desire to know how to act in such circumstances? Jesus ministered occasionally to the temporal wants of men, and labored continually to promote their spiritual good. Is man popular? So was Jesus; and he used his influence to purify his Father's house. Is man forsaken by his last friend? So was Jesus; and he upbraided and murmured not, but sought consolation in communion with the Father. Does man visit and dine with the learned, and the religious formalists of the age? So did Jesus; and in his conversation he maintained the claims of spiritual religion, and reproved man's hypocrisy and formality. Does man sit down in the cottage of the poor? So did Jesus; and he encouraged and comforted the inmates with spiritual instruction. Is man present when a group of friends are assembled on an occasion which warrants innocent enjoyment? So was Jesus; and he approved their social pleasures. Is man called to sympathize with those in affliction? So was Jesus; and *Jesus wept!* Thus by land and by sea, in all places and under all circumstances, wherever any of earth's children are called to act, Jesus—the model man—is seen, living and moving before them; and his voice falls upon their ear with the mingled cadence of authority and encouragement—"Follow me!"

The demonstration, then, is manifest, that through the medium of Jesus Christ man has received a perfect system of instruction; and a final and perfect revelation of duty to God and man could be given in no other way.

Chapter XI.

CONCERNING SOME OF THE PECULIAR PROOFS OF THE MESSIAHSHIP OF CHRIST.

We have now arrived at a point in our subject where the light of history will aid in our investigations. The facts which history furnishes, and which will elucidate the present point of inquiry, are the following:

First, the Jewish prophets lived and wrote centuries before the period in which Jesus appeared in Judea. This fact is as certain as any other item of human knowledge.

A second fact is: The Jews, about the time of Christ's appearance, expected, with more earnestness and desire than usual, the appearance of their Messiah, who, they supposed, would deliver them from subjection to Gentile nations, and place the Jewish power in the ascendant among the nations of the earth. They generally supposed that, as a king, he would reign with great dignity and power; and, as a priest, preside over, not abrogate, the ceremonial law. Although some of the common people may have had some understanding of the true nature of the Messiah's kingdom, yet the prominent men of the nation, and the great body of the people of all classes, were not expecting that the kingdom of Christ would be purely spiritual, but that it would be mainly temporal. And, indeed, it was necessary that they should not have a clear conception of the worth and spirituality of the Messiah's dispensation, previously to his coming; because if they had had such a conception, the imperfections and darkness of their own dispensation would not have been borne. It is contrary to the nature of mind, when it is enlightened, to delight in, and employ itself longer about, the preparatory steps that led it to the light.

The facts in the case, then, were: First, the prophets lived and wrote centuries before the era of Christ; and, second, on account of intimations, or supposed intimations, in their prophecies, the Jews were expecting the Messiah about the time that Jesus appeared in Judea. With the question concerning the inspiration of the prophets we have nothing to do. Whether they were inspired or not, their books contained the matter upon which the Jews founded their expectation of the appearance of the Messiah. With the question how the Jews could mistake the character of the Messiah we have nothing to do, although the solution of the question would not be difficult. The simple facts which require attention are: The prophecies existed; and in those prophecies a Ruler was spoken of, of most exalted character, whose dominion would be triumphant, universal, and endless; whose doctrines would be pure and spiritual, and whose administration would be a blessing, not only to the Jews, but also to the Gentiles; and yet his life would be humble, and not suited to the feeling of the Jews; his sufferings extreme; and that he would terminate the old dispensation, and die for the sins of the people.*

Now, in view of these facts, *in what character would the true Messiah appear when he assumed his duties as the Instructor of mankind?*

If he had appeared and conformed to the views which the Jews entertained of a temporal Messiah, it would have been direct evidence that he was an impostor; because the Jewish views of his character and reign, as all can now see, were selfish, ambitious, imperfect, and partial. Now, a teacher sent from God to give the world a perfect religion could not conform to such views; but an impostor, from the nature of the case, could have conformed to no other standard than the views of the people. If an impostor wished to pass himself upon the Jews as their Messiah, he must assume that character and conform to that conduct which he knew they expected in their Messiah. For an impostor to assume a different character from that which he knew the nation expected their Messiah would bear, would have been to use means to frustrate his own plans, which would be impossible; because man can not have a governing desire for the attainment of an end, and at the same time use means which he knows will frustrate the accomplishment of his own object. An impostor, therefore, in the state

---

* Is. liii; Dan. ix, 24–27; Micah v, 1, 2; Mal. iii, 1–3; Zech. ix, 9, 10; Is. ix, 1–10.

of expectancy which existed at that time in Judea, could not do otherwise than conform himself to the character which the nation were expecting their Messiah would possess.

Mark the two points. The prophets gave a delineation of the character, life, and death of the Messiah. This delineation the Jews misinterpreted, or applied to several individuals; so that they were expecting in their Messiah a character entirely different from that described by the prophets.

Now, mark the application of these points. If Christ had conformed to the views of the Jews, there would have been three direct testimonies that he was not from God: 1. Because their views were partial, prejudiced, wicked; 2. He could not have conformed to their views and sustain at the same time the character of a perfect instructor; * 3. He would not have fulfilled the predictions of the prophets concerning him. But, on the other hand, if he conformed to the prophets, and assumed the character of a perfect teacher, his rejection by the Jews was absolutely certain.† It follows, therefore, legitimately and conclusively, that Jesus Christ was the Messiah of God,

---

* See chap. x.

† The fact that Jesus conformed to the prophets, established the truth of the prophecies; because, by conforming to them, he suffered death; while by his death, in accordance with the prophets, the world gained the evidence that he was the true Messiah. To give life as a testimony to falsehood is impossible, either in a good or in an evil being.

because he pursued that course which would, from the nature of the case, result in his rejection by the nation; which conduct, in an impostor, would be impossible, but in the true Messiah it was the necessary course.

But, further, it was necessary that Jesus should establish his claim as the Messiah by miraculous agency.* But owing to the peculiar state of the Jewish nation at that time, there would be great difficulty in doing this, for the following reasons: If he, as Moses did, had come publicly before the nation at Jerusalem, and by miracles of great power, frequently repeated and extending their influence throughout all the land, had forced conviction upon the minds of all the Jews that he was the true Messiah, the immediate and inevitable result would have been, that they would have raised one universal revolt against the Roman power, and would have hurried the Savior of sinners into the office of King of the Jews, and then bowed down to him as the temporal sovereign of the Jewish nation. But, notwithstanding this error of the Jews and the results to which it would directly tend, still it would be necessary, in order to meet the constitution of things, that Christ should manifest, by exhibitions of miraculous power, the credentials attesting the divinity of his mission. The inquiry, then, arises, *How could Jesus perform miracles, and at the same time prevent revolt in the nation?*

The circumstances of the case would render it necessary that his miracles should not be attended by

---

* See chap. iii: "On Miracles."

that publicity and power which would lead those who had the influence of the nation in their hands, and who were blind to the true design of his mission, into revolt and destruction. It was likewise necessary, on the other hand, that they should be sufficiently frequent and of sufficient power to convince the candid who witnessed them that they were the seal of heaven to the mission of Jesus. When Christ wrought miracles, therefore, he would have to aim at one end, and endeavor to prevent another: the end aimed at, that the impression might be made on honest minds that he was the true Messiah; the end avoided, that the rulers of the nation might not, on account of his mighty miracles, rally round him as their temporal king, and thus hurry themselves and their nation to premature destruction.

Now, the character and conduct of Jesus accords entirely with the foregoing deductions, made out from undoubted historical facts. That he performed many miracles, and yet suppressed their extensive publicity, is frequently noticed in the New Testament. Jesus, therefore, had the peculiar marks of the true Messiah; and, in view of the peculiar condition of the Jewish nation at that time, the true Messiah could have assumed no other character and pursued no other course of conduct than that exhibited in the life of Christ.*

---

* Another item might be added to this demonstration, showing that in order to the ultimation of the Plan of Salvation, it was necessary that Jesus should so manifest himself and manage his ministry, that a part of the Jews should receive him as the Messiah, and a part reject him.

Chapter XII.

CONCERNING THE CONDITION IN LIFE WHICH IT WAS NECESSARY THE MESSIAH SHOULD ASSUME, IN ORDER TO BENEFIT THE HUMAN FAMILY IN THE GREATEST DEGREE BY HIS EXAMPLE AND INSTRUCTIONS.

SELFISHNESS is a fundamental evil of human nature, the existence of which is acknowledged by all men. It is not an evil which belongs to any one class of human society. It is generic, and moves all ranks; only each individual looks upon those who stand next or near him in society, and desires equality with, or superiority over, them in wealth or popularity or power. The law of reason and of God requires that men should endeavor to elevate those below them up to their own condition; selfishness is the opposite principle, which urges men to elevate themselves over others. If the militia captain could follow the desires of his nature, and ascend from one condition to another until he stood upon the floor of the Senate chamber, he would find that the desire which led him to take the first step, had only increased its power by gratification, and was still goading him on to rise higher; and he would stop nowhere, while life lasted, until he perceived further efforts useless or dangerous. This selfish pride and desire for self-aggrandizement is detrimental both to the individual and the social interests of men. Wherever selfish ambition exists in any degree of strength, it generates misery to the individual and to others about him. There are not, perhaps, any more miserable men in the world than are some of those who have gained to some extent the object of their ambition, and are seated in the halls of legislation. Their minds are constantly anxious in making some effort or devising some plan by which they may promote schemes in which they are engaged. And every time the hopes of one are realized, the stings of envy and jealousy and concealed hate rankle in the bosoms of some others. In the humbler walks of life the evil exists, perhaps, in a less degree; but still it exists; and its existence is the bane of human happiness, and the cause of human guilt.

Now, this wicked desire of human nature to aspire after elevated worldly condition, rather than after usefulness of life and goodness of heart, would be either fostered or checked by the condition in life which the Messiah assumed among men. In proportion as his condition was elevated, pride and the desire of elevation would be fostered in the hearts of his followers. In proportion as his condition was humble and depressed, pride of heart would be checked in all those who received and honored him as their master and teacher.*

Suppose that the Messiah had presented himself in the condition anticipated by the Jews, surrounded by

---

* See chap. v.

the pomp and parade of a powerful temporal prince, sustaining the earthly dignity and splendor of the ancient monarchs of the dynasty of David. Now, had such a Messiah appeared in Judea, it is perfectly certain, from the character of human nature, that his earthly circumstances would have a tendency to cherish in the people, as a nation and as individuals, the bad principles of pride and ambition. Worldly pomp and circumstance would have had the sanction of the highest authority in the person of their Messiah; and it would have induced the desire in all hearts to elevate themselves as nearly as possible to his temporal condition. The pride of the human heart would have been fostered and not humbled. Instead of causing the middle walks of life to be grateful and contented in their condition, it would have produced in them an anxiety to stretch themselves upwards; and instead of causing those already elevated to fellowship and benefit the worthy poor, it would have caused them to have no sympathy for any of the human family in low estate, because theirs was a condition the opposite of that assumed by the great model which they loved and admired; and instead of causing the poor to feel a greater degree of contentment, and to avoid repining at their lot, the circumstances of the Messiah would have deepened their dejection and rendered them less happy in their depressed condition, because their condition would hinder them from approach to, or fellowship with, the heaven-sent Instructor. A teacher, therefore, believed to be from heaven, who should assume an elevated condition in the world, instead of being a spiritual blessing to the whole family of man, by promoting in their bosoms humility and sympathy for each other, would have been a spiritual curse, by producing haughtiness and hardness of heart in the rich, ambition in the middle classes, and hopeless dejection in the poor.

Suppose the Messiah had come in the character which the Greeks admired; that, assuming the seat of the philosophers, he had startled the learned world by disclosing to them new and sublime truths. Suppose he had, by the power of far-reaching intellect, answered all the questions and solved all the difficulties which perplexed the minds of the disciples of the Porch and the Academy. In such a case his instructions would have been adapted to satisfy the minds of a few gifted individuals; but they would not have been adapted to benefit the minds of many, nor the heart of any of the great mass of mankind. Vain of their wisdom already, the character of the Messiah would have been adapted to make the philosophers more so; and instead of blessing them, by humbling their pride and giving them a sympathy with their fellow-men, it would have led them and their admirers to look upon those who were not endowed with superior mental qualities as an inferior class of men.

But if the Messiah could not have appeared in the condition desired by the Jews, nor in that admired by the Gentiles, the inquiry arises, What condition in life would it be necessary that the Messiah should assume in order to benefit the human family in the highest degree by the influence of that condition? In view of the foregoing deductions the solution is obvious: *In that condition which would have the most direct influence to destroy selfishness and pride in the human heart, and to foster, in their stead, humility, contentment, and benevolence.*

Now, in view of this result, deduced directly from the acknowledged character of human nature, turn your attention to the earthly circumstances of Jesus, and see how directly he brought the whole weight of his condition in life to bear against selfishness and pride of heart. He was born in the lowest possible circumstances. His life was a constant rebuke to every ambitious and proud feeling of the human heart, and his death was one esteemed by men the most ignominious. No one who openly acknowledged and had fellowship with Jesus of Nazareth as his Teacher and Master, could do so until the natural pride of his nature was subdued. It was impossible for a man to find fellowship with Jesus unless he humbled himself, because in no other state could his feelings meet those of Christ. "Take my yoke upon you," said Jesus, "and learn of me, for I am meek and lowly in heart, and ye shall find rest for your souls."

Thus did Jesus place himself in a condition which rendered humility absolutely necessary in order to sympathy with him—in the condition directly opposed to pride of heart, one of the most insidious enemies of man's happiness and usefulness. And as it is an acknowledged and experimental fact that the soul finds rest only in meekness, and never in selfishness and pride of mind, therefore the demonstration is perfect, that Christ assumed the only condition which it was possible for him to assume, and thereby destroy pride and misery, and produce humility and peace, in human bosoms.

Profane history and the New Testament Scriptures confirm the foregoing views. Tacitus, speaking of the primitive Christians, alludes to them with marked contempt as the followers of one who had been crucified. His manner evinces clearly not only his own feelings, but it is a good index to the feelings of a majority of the people of that proud and idolatrous age; and it establishes beyond all controversy the fact that no one could declare himself a follower of Christ until, for truth and for Christ's sake, he was willing to be considered base in the estimation of the world. The elegant Pliny likewise bears direct testimony to the humility and integrity of life which characterized the early disciples of Christ.

A great number of passages in the New Testament confirm the preceding views. It is only necessary to say that the apostles understood not only the effect of their Lord's circumstances, in life and death, upon the minds of men, but they understood likewise the philosophy and the necessity of the case. Says Paul: "It became [or was expedient for] him, for whom are all things, and by whom are all things, in bringing many sons unto glory, to make the captain of their salvation perfect through suffering; for both he that sanctifieth and they who are sanctified are all of one, for which cause he is not ashamed to call them brethren." That is, the humble and self-denying life and death of Jesus was necessary, because it would have a sanctifying effect in counteracting the evils in the hearts of men. It was necessary for him to become their brother man, and assume a certain character and condition, in order that by their becoming one with him they might be sanctified and made happy and useful.

Thus while the Jews required a sign and the Greeks sought after wisdom, the apostles preached Christ crucified, understanding the philosophy, the efficiency, and the necessity of their doctrine. And so long as the world lasts, every man who reads the New Testament, whether saint or sinner, will be penetrated with the conviction that a vain, aspiring, selfish spirit is incompatible with the religion of Jesus.

Chapter XIII.

CONCERNING THE ESSENTIAL PRINCIPLES WHICH MUST, ACCORDING TO THE NATURE OF THINGS, LIE AT THE FOUNDATION OF THE INSTRUCTION OF CHRIST.

The Messiah having come in the proper character, displayed the proper credentials, and assumed the necessary condition, the question arises, What may we learn from the character of God and the nature of man concerning the fundamental principles which would govern the teaching of Jesus?

God is righteous and benevolent; it therefore follows that he would connect happiness with righteousness and goodness in his creatures. Were he to do otherwise it would be causing the happiness of men to arise from a character different from his own, which, as God is good, would be impossible, because it would be wicked.

Further, man is so constituted that, as a matter of fact, his true happiness depends upon righteousness of life and benevolence of heart. When his will accords with his knowledge of duty, or when he acts as he knows is right towards God and his fellow-men, there is peace and even complacency of conscience. Peace and complacency of conscience is the happiness which, according to man's moral constitution, arises from righteousness, or right acting, in life. And when man exercises benevolent feeling, has love in his heart to God and men, this exercise of benevolent affection produces happiness. Now, there can be no such thing as happiness of spirit except it arises from these sources. And when these sources are full and flowing, and thus unite together; when there is perfect love and a perfect life, the soul is rendered happy. A single unrighteous act of will or malevolent feeling of heart will destroy this happiness; a single emotion of hatred or ill-will, or a single evil act, known to be such, towards any of God's creatures, will destroy the peace of the soul. Even hatred to an enemy, or the desire of revenge, or any emotion but good-will, injures the soul's happiness.

Thus, in constituting the human soul, God, in accordance with his own character, has caused its happiness to depend upon righteousness and goodness.

Now, then, a teacher sent from God must recognize these fundamental principles, and give his instruction in view of them. The happiness of the human soul—which is its *life*, its first and best and only good—could be produced in no other way. The whole force, therefore, of divine instruction would be designed and adapted to accomplish this necessary end. The legitimate development of God's nature, exercised towards man, would produce such instructions and such an example; and the best good of the human soul rendered it necessary that they should be given.

It is not said that, as in the schools of philosophy,

the constant inquiry and search should be for the "greatest good." The very effort to obtain happiness in this way would destroy its existence. Happiness is not objective but subjective; no direct effort could gain it; it is the *result* of the right action of the moral powers. It would not be necessary, therefore, that those instructed should even understand the principles which governed their instructor. It would be sufficient if the instruction was designed and adapted to promote righteousness and goodness: then happiness of the soul would follow as a result, whether or not the recipient of the instruction understood the principles which governed his teacher.

Now, the whole power of Christ's instruction was directed to this point. It was distinguished in this respect from all other instruction ever given to mankind: I say unto you, love your enemies. Do good to them that despitefully use you. Be anxious about no worldly good. The weightier matters of the law are *righteousness* and the *love of God*. Love and obey God, and love and do good to your neighbor; this is the law and the prophets. Seek first the kingdom of heaven and its righteousness, and all other things will be added to you. That is, seek first righteousness and the love of God, and the necessary result will grow out of these exercises; happiness, or life, will be added as a consequence.

Thus was the whole force of the Savior's teaching and example designed and adapted to produce righteousness and benevolence; and as these are the only exercises from which man's true happiness can arise, it follows that the principles involved in the instruction of Christ, connecting happiness with holiness, are the only principles which can, in accordance with the character of God and the constitution of man, produce the greatest good of the human soul. Jesus, therefore, was the Christ of God; because the Christ of God could found his instructions on no other principles: the principles which are fundamental in his teaching being those which alone can produce the happiness of the soul in accordance with its own moral nature, and in accordance with the moral character of God.

Chapter XIV.

CONCERNING FAITH, AS THE EXERCISE THROUGH WHICH TRUTH REACHES AND AFFECTS THE SOUL.

WHEN Christ, man's perfect and spiritual instructor, had come, and introduced the great doctrines of the spiritual dispensation, the next necessary step in the process was, that those truths should be brought to impress the soul and influence the life, and so produce their proper effects upon human nature. The inquiry then presents itself, *In what way could the truths of the Gospel be brought into efficient contact with the soul of man?*

There are but two ways in which truth can be brought into contact with the mind; the one is sometimes called knowledge, the other faith or belief of testimony. In the earlier and ruder ages men were necessarily moved more by knowledge, derived from their own observation and experience through the medium of their senses; but as mankind increased in number, important truth was conveyed by one man or one generation communicating their experience, and another man or another generation receiving it by belief in their testimony. Perception and faith are the only modes by which truth can be brought into contact with the soul; and their effects are nearly the same upon man's conduct and feelings, with the following remarkable exception: Facts which are the subjects of personal observation, every time they are experienced, the effect upon the soul grows less; while on the contrary, those facts which are received by faith produce, every time they are realized, a greater effect upon the soul. By constant sight, the effect of objects seen grows less; by constant faith, the effect of objects believed in grows greater. The probable reason of this is, that personal observation does not admit of the influence of the imagination in impressing the fact; while unseen objects, realized by faith, have the auxiliary aid of the imagination, not to exaggerate them, but to clothe them with living colors, and impress them upon the heart. Whether this be the reason or not, the fact is true, that the more frequently we *see* the less we *feel* the power of an object; while the more frequently we dwell upon an object by faith, the more we feel its power. This being true, it follows that faith would be the method best adapted to bring the sublime truths of the new dispensation to bear upon the souls of men. And, further, as the dispensation is spiritual, and has relation to unseen and eternal things, faith becomes the only medium through which they can be conveyed to the soul.

Furthermore, man is so constituted that his faith, or belief, has an influence, not only over his conduct in life, but likewise over the character and action of the moral powers of the soul.

Faith governs the *Conscience.*

We have said, in another place, that a true conscience depends upon a true faith. No proposition in morals is more plain. It is not our design to inquire what leads, or has led, men to a wrong faith. Whatever may be the cause of any particular belief, it is incontrovertible that if a man believes a thing to be right, conscience can not condemn an act performed in view of that belief. Conscience is so modified and guided by a man's faith that it will sanction and command an act in one man which it will forbid and condemn in another. A Catholic believes that he ought to pray to the Virgin Mary to intercede for him with God; and if a good Catholic were to neglect his *dulia* to the saints, his conscience would smite him, until, in some instances, he confesses his sins with tears. Now, if a good Protestant were to pray to saints, or to any other being but God, his conscience would smite him for doing that which the conscience of the Catholic smote him for not doing. So the heathen mother will conscientiously throw her infant into the Ganges or under the wheels of Juggernaut, while the conscience of a Christian mother would convict her of murder were she to do the same act. Conscience seldom convicts those that Christians call impenitent persons for neglecting to pray, while the moment a man becomes a true believer he will be convicted of guilt if he neglects the duty. So certainly and so clearly is it true, that a man's conscience is governed by his faith.

Faith governs the *Affections*.

As man is constituted, no power in the universe can move his affections to an object until he believes that the object possesses some loveliness or excellency of character. The heart is affected just as much by the goodness of another if we *believe* that goodness to exist as it would be if we *knew* that it existed. No matter, in the case of the affections, whether the object in reality possesses the good qualities or not: if they are fully believed to exist, the affections will act just as certainly as though they really did exist. The affections are constituted to be governed by faith. And they act most powerfully, as was demonstrated in a previous chapter, in view of good qualities existing in another, who under certain circumstances exercises those qualities towards us. The fact, then, is apparent, that the conduct of man's life is influenced by what he believes; and especially that the character and action of the moral powers of his nature are governed by the principle of faith.

Another most important fact in connection with this subject is, that a man's interests, temporal and spiritual, depend upon *what* he believes. The nature of man and the nature of things are so constituted that the belief of falsehood always destroys man's interests, temporal or spiritual, and the belief of truth invariably guides man right, and secures his best and highest good.

Perhaps the most absurd and injurious adage that has ever gained currency among mankind is, that "it is no difference what a man believes, if he only be sincere." Now, the truth is, that the more sincerely a man believes falsehood, the more destructive it is to all his interests for time and eternity. This statement can be confirmed in every mind beyond the reach of doubt.

First: The influence of believing falsehood on temporal and social interests.

We will state some cases of common and constant occurrence, in order that the principle may be made obvious:

A gentleman of property and the highest respectability, in the course of his business transactions, became acquainted with an individual, who, as the event showed, was a man destitute in a great degree of a conscientious regard for truth. The persuasions and false representations of this man led the gentleman referred to, to embark almost his entire fortune with him in speculations in which he was at that time engaged. While this matter was in progress, the friends of the gentleman called upon him, and stated their doubts of the individual's integrity who solicited his confidence, and likewise of the success of the enterprises in which he was solicited to engage. The advice of his friends was rejected. He placed confidence in the false statements of the individual referred to; he acted upon those statements, and was consequently involved in pecuniary distress. In this case the gentleman not only sincerely believed the falsehood to be the truth, but he had good motives in relation to the object which he desired to accomplish.

He was a benevolent man. He had expended considerable sums for charitable and religious uses, and his desire was, by the increase of his property, to be enabled to accomplish greater good. In this case he was injured, likewise, by believing what others did not believe. The individual who seduced him into the speculation had endeavored to lead others to take the same views and to act in the same way. They did not believe the falsehood, and were, consequently, saved; he believed, and was, consequently ruined.

When the English army under Harold, and the Norman under William the Conquerer, were set in array for that fearful conflict which decided the fate of the two armies and the political destinies of Great Britain, William, perceiving that he could not, by a fair attack, move the solid columns of the English ranks, had recourse to a false movement, in order to gain the victory. He gave orders that one flank of his army should feign to be flying from the field in disorder. The officers of the English army believed the falsehood, pursued them, and were cut off. A second time, a false movement was made in another part of the field. The English again believed, pursued, and were cut off. By these movements the fortunes of the day were determined. Although the English had the evidence of their senses, yet they were led to believe a falsehood: they acted in view of it. The consequence was the destruction of a great part of their army, and the establishment of the Norman power in England.

How often does it occur that the young female, possessing warm affections and being inexperienced in the wiles of villains, is led to believe falsehood, which destroys her prospects and her happiness while life lasts! Under other circumstances she might have been virtuous, useful, happy. By false indications of affection her heart is won; by false promises of faithfulness and future good her assent to marry is gained; and then, when too late, she discovers that her husband is a villain, and she is forsaken, with a broken heart, to the cold sympathies of a selfish world. No matter how many hearts besides her own are broken by her error! No matter how sincere, or how guileless, or how young: she sincerely believed the falsehood, and is thereby ruined. Nothing in heaven or on earth will avert the consequences. If she had doubted, she would have been saved. She believed, and is consigned to sorrow till she sinks into her grave.

Second: The belief of falsehood in relation to spiritual things destroys man's spiritual interests.

It is an incontrovertible fact that the whole heathen world, ancient and modern, have believed in and worshiped unholy beings as gods. Now, from the necessities of the case, as demonstrated in the introductory chapter, the worshiper becomes assimilated to the character of the object worshiped. In consequence of believing falsehood concerning the character of God, all heathendom, at the present hour, is filled with ignorance, impurity, and crime. As a mass of corruption spreads contagion and death among all those who approach it, so certainly does the worship of unholy beings attaint the soul, and spread moral corruption through the world. "Can a man take coals into his bosom and not be burned?" Neither can the soul hold communion with beings believed to be unholy and not itself become corrupt. The fact is so plain that it is not necessary to detail again the impurities, the vices, the tortures, the self-murders, and the unnatural affections of the heathen world, in order to show the deadly evils, both to the body and soul, which arise from the belief of falsehood in relation to spiritual things. It must be obvious to every one that if the heathen believed in one holy and benevolent God, their abominable and cruel rites would cease. It follows, therefore, that it is the belief of falsehood that causes their ignorance and corruption.

Thus it is invariably and eternally true that the belief of truth will lead a man right, and secure his temporal, spiritual, and eternal interests; and, on the contrary, the belief of falsehood will lead a man wrong, and destroy his interests in relation to whatever the falsehood pertains, whether it be temporal or eternal.

The preceding premises being established, the following conclusions result:

1. That the entire man, in his body and soul, his actions and moral feelings, is governed by what he believes; and that, in relation to things that should have a constantly increasing influence over the spirit, faith is a more powerful actuating cause than sight,

because the one gains while the other loses power over the soul by repetition.

2. That the belief of falsehood concerning any human interest is fatally injurious, while the belief of truth is eternally beneficial; and that the more sincerely any one believes error, the more certainly he destroys his interests, whether temporal or spiritual; while, on the contrary, the more sincerely a man believes truth, the more certainly and powerfully are his interests advanced. The living God has connected evil with the belief of falsehood, and good with the belief of truth; it is a part of the constitutional law of the moral universe, and there is no power in existence that will stop the consequence from following the antecedent.

3. Mark it: That doctrine which rectifies the conscience, purifies the heart, and produces love to God and men, *is necessarily true:* because, as it has been demonstrated that righteousness and benevolence is the greatest good of the soul, and likewise that the greatest good must depend on the belief of truth, therefore the conclusion is inevitable, that that doctrine which, being believed, destroys sin in the heart and life of man, and produces righteousness and benevolence, is the truth of God. No matter whether men can comprehend all its depths and relations or not: if it destroys sin wherever it takes effect by faith, and makes happiness grow out of *right living* and *right loving*, from the constitution of things—from the character of God, from the nature of man—that doctrine

is the TRUTH OF GOD. And that doctrine which hinders this result, or produces a contrary result, is the falsehood of the devil.*

4. Therefore Christ laid, at the foundation of the Christian system, this vital and necessary principle: " He that believeth and is baptized shall be saved, and he that believeth not shall be damned;" saved in accordance with the moral constitution of the universe, and damned from the absolute necessities existing in the nature of things.

---

* John viii, 44.

Chapter XV.

CONCERNING THE MANIFESTATIONS OF GOD WHICH WOULD BE NECESSARY, UNDER THE NEW AND SPIRITUAL DISPENSATION, TO PRODUCE IN THE SOUL OF MAN AFFECTIONATE OBEDIENCE.

MAN's mental and moral constitution was the same under the New as under the Old Testament dispensation. The same methods, therefore, which were adapted to move man's nature under the one, would be adapted to do so under the other. The difference between the two dispensations was: the first was a preparatory dispensation, its manifestations, for the most part, being seen and temporal; the second, a perfect system of truth, spiritual in its character and in the method of its communication. But whether the truths were temporal or spiritual, and whether they were brought to view by faith or sight, in order to produce a given effect upon the soul or any of its powers, the same methods under all dispensations would be necessary, varied only to suit the advancement of the mind in knowledge, the differences existing in the habits and circumstances of men and the character of the dispensation to be introduced. For instance, under one dispensation—it being in a great measure temporal, preparatory, and imperfect—love might be produced by making men feel temporal want, and by God granting temporal benefits; while under a spiritual and universal system men must likewise feel the want and receive the benefit, in order to love; but the want felt and the benefit conferred must be of a spiritual character.

Under all dispensations, an essential requisite, after the way for its introduction was prepared, would be such manifestations of God to men as would produce love in the human heart for the object of worship and obedience. "Love the Lord thy God with all thy heart" is the first great law of the universe; and God can not be honored, nor man made happy, unless his obedience be actuated by love to the object of obedience.* Now, the manifestations of mercy under the old dispensation were mainly temporal in their character, and limited in their application to the Jews. But God's special goodness to them could not produce love in the hearts of the Gentiles. The manifestations in Egypt were, therefore, neither adapted in their character nor in the extent of their design, to the spiritual and universal religion of Jesus Christ. But one part of the Mosaic economy was universal and immutable in its character. The moral law is the same forever in its application to all intelligent beings in the universe. It is plain to reason that whatever means may be adapted to bring men to rectitude of conduct, or to pardon them for offenses, the rule of right itself, founded upon the justice and holiness and

---

* See chap. iv, on "Affectionate Obedience."

sustained by the conscience of the Eternal, must be immutable and eternal as its author; and the means, manifestations, and influences under the different dispensations are expedients of mercy, designed and adapted to bring men to act in conformity with its requirements.

How, then, under the new dispensation, and in conformity with its spiritual and universal character, could love for God be produced in the human heart?

We will here, again, as the subject in hand is most important, notice some of the conditions upon which affection for an object may be produced in the heart.

The will is influenced by motives and by affection; and all acts of will produced entirely by pure affection are disinterested acts. There is, probably, no one living who has attained to maturity of years, but has, at some period of life, felt affection for another, so that it was more gratifying to please the object of his affection than to please himself. Love for another always influences the will to do those things which please the object loved; and the acts which proceed from affection are disinterested, not being done with any selfish end in view, but to conform to the will and meet the desires of another. The moment the affections are fixed upon an object, the will is drawn into union with the will of the object loved; and if that object be regarded as superior, in proportion as he rises above us in the scale of being, to obey his will and secure his regard becomes a spontaneous volition of the soul; and the pleasure that arises from affectionate compliance with the will of a worthy and loved object does not arise because it is sought for, but from the constitution the Maker has given to the human soul; it is the result of its activity, produced in accordance with the law of love.

All happy obedience must arise from affection exercised towards the object obeyed. Obedience which arises from affection blesses the spirit which yields it, if the conscience approve of the object obeyed; while, on the contrary, no being can be happy in obeying one whom he does not love. To obey a parent or to obey God from interested motives would be sin. The devil might be obeyed for the same reasons. All enlightened minds agree to what the Bible confirms, and what reason can clearly perceive without argument, that love for God is essential to every act of religious duty. To tender obedience or homage to God while we had no love for him in our hearts would be dishonorable to the Maker, and doing violence to our own nature.

When an object presents itself to the attention, whose character engages the heart, then the affections flow out, and the soul acts sweetly in this new relation. There is a bond of sympathy between the hearts of the two beings, and those things which affect the one affect the other, in proportion to the strength of the cherished affection. One meets the desires and conforms to the will of the other, not from a sense of obligation merely, but from choice. And in thus giving and receiving affection, the soul experiences its highest enjoyment, its greatest good; and when the understanding perceives in the object loved perfections of the highest character, and affection of the purest kind for those that love him, the conscience sanctions the action of the heart and the obedience of the will, and all the moral powers of the soul unite in happy and harmonious action.

We return, now, to the problem: Under the spiritual dispensation of Christ, how could the affections of the soul be awakened by faith, and fixed upon God, their proper object?

The principle has been stated, which every one will recognize as true in his own experience, that the more we feel the want of a benefactor, temporal or spiritual, and the more we feel our inability to rescue ourselves from existing difficulties and impending dangers, the more grateful love will the heart feel for the being who, moved by kindness, and in despite of personal sacrifices, interposes to assist and save us.

Under the Old Testament dispensation, the affections of the Israelites were educed and fixed upon God in accordance with this law of the soul. They were placed in circumstances of abject need; and from this condition of suffering and sorrow God delivered them, and thus drew their hearts to himself. Now, the Jews, as has been noticed, supposed that the Messiah would appear, and again confer upon them similar favors, by delivering them from their state of dependence and subjection as a nation. But a temporal deliverance of this kind, as has been shown, was not consistent with the design of Christ's perfect and spiritual dispensation, which was designed to save men from sin and spiritual bondage, and restore them to spiritual happiness by restoring them to affectionate obedience to the only living and true God.

The inquiry then presents itself: As a feeling of want was necessary in order that the soul might love the being that supplied that want, and as Jesus came to bestow spiritual mercies upon mankind, *How could men be brought to feel the want of a spiritual Benefactor and Savior?*

Allow the thought to be repeated again: According to the constitution which God has given the soul, it must feel the want of spiritual mercies before it can feel love for the giver of those mercies; and just in proportion as the soul feels its lost, guilty, and dangerous condition, in the same proportion will it exercise love to the being who grants spiritual favor and salvation. How, then, could the spiritual want be produced in the souls of men in order that they might love the spiritual benefactor?

Not by temporal bondage and temporal suffering, because these would lead men to desire a temporal deliverance. The only possible way by which man could be made to hope for and appreciate spiritual mercies and to love a spiritual deliverer, would be to produce a conviction in the soul itself of its evil condition, its danger as a spiritual being, and its inability, unaided, to satisfy the requirements of a *spiritual law*, or to escape its just and spiritual penalty. If man could be made to perceive that he was guilty and needy; that his soul was under the condemnation of the holy law of a holy God, he would then, necessarily, feel the need of a deliverance from sin and its consequences; and in this way only could the soul of man be led to appreciate spiritual mercies or love a spiritual benefactor.

Mark another fact in connection with the foregoing, which is to be especially noticed, and which will be developed fully in subsequent pages: the greater the kindness and self-denial of a benefactor manifested in our behalf, the warmer and the stronger will be the affection which his goodness will produce in the human heart.

Here, then, are two facts growing out of the constitution of human nature: First, the soul must feel its evil and lost estate, as the prerequisite condition upon which alone it can love a deliverer; second, the degree of kindness and self-denial in a benefactor, temporal or spiritual, graduates the degree of affection and gratitude that will be awakened for him.

Now, in view of these necessary conditions, mark the means which God has used, and the manifestations which he has made of himself, in order to secure the supreme love of the human soul.

In the first place, the soul is brought to see and feel its evil and lost condition, and its need of deliverance.

At the advent of Jesus the Roman world was in precisely the condition which was necessary to prepare it for his doctrines. The Jews had the moral law written in their Scriptures, and recognized it as the will of Jehovah; and the Gentiles had its requirements, concerning their duty to each other and their duty to worship, written upon their hearts. Both the doctors among the Jews and the schools of philosophy among the Gentiles, especially those of the Stoics, taught the obligatory nature of many of the important moral duties which man owes to man. No period in the history of the heathen mind ever existed, before or since, when man's relations to man were so clearly perceived.* The Jews, however, had these advantages, that while the few intelligent Gentiles received the instruction of the philosophers in relation to morals as truth, it was truth without any higher sanction than that of having been spoken by wise men, and therefore it contained in itself no authority or weight of obligation to bind the conscience; while they had the moral law as a rule of duty, sanctioned by the authority and infinite justice of Jehovah. Thus the moral virtues assumed the sanction of religious duties; and they had not only the moral precepts thus sanctioned, but, having been taught the true character of God, their religious duties were likewise united in the same sacred Decalogue.

There was, however, in the application of the law one most important and vital mistake in relation to

---

* For the views of the different schools of Grecian and Roman philosophy at this period, and the amount of their indebtedness to the Jewish Scriptures, see Enfield's History of Philosophy.

what constituted human guilt. The moral law was generally applied as the civil law, not to the acts of the spirit, but to the acts of the body. It was applied to the external conduct of men, not to the internal life. If there was conformity to the letter of the law in external manners, there was a fulfillment, in the eyes of the Jew and the Gentile, of the highest claims that God or man held upon the spirit. No matter how dark or damning were the exercises of the soul: if it only kept its sin in its own habitation, and did not develop it in action, the penalty of the law was not laid to its charge. The character of the spirit itself might be criminal, and all its exercises of thought and feeling sensual and selfish, yet if it added hypocrisy to its guilt, and maintained an outward conformity to the law—a conformity itself produced by selfishness—man judged himself, and others adjudged him, guiltless. Man could not, therefore, understand his own guilt as a spiritual being, nor feel his condemned and lost condition, until the requirements of the holy law were applied to the exercises of his soul.

Now, Jesus applied the divine law directly to the soul, and laid its obligation upon the movements of the will, and the desires. He taught that all wrong thoughts and feelings were acts of transgression against God, and as such would be visited with the penalty of the divine law. Thus he made the law spiritual and its penalty spiritual, and appealing to the authority of the supreme God, he laid its claims upon the naked soul. He entered the secret recesses of the spirit's tabernacle; he flashed the light of the divine law upon the awful secrets known only to the soul itself; and with the voice of God he spoke to the "I" of the mind: Thou shalt not *will,* nor *desire,* nor *feel* wickedly!

When he had thus shown that all the wrong exercises of the soul were sin against God, and that the soul was in a guilty condition, under the condemnation of the divine law, he then directed the attention to the spiritual consequences of this guilt. These he declared to be exclusion from the kingdom and presence of God, and penalty which involved either endless spiritual suffering or destruction of the soul itself. The punishment which he declared to be impending over the unbelieving and impenitent spirit, he portrayed by using all those figures which would lead men to apprehend the most fearful and unmitigated spiritual misery.

Before the impenitent and unpardoned sinner there was the destruction of the soul and body in hell; consignment to a state of darkness, where the worm dieth not, and the fire is not quenched; cursed, and banished from God into everlasting fire, prepared for the devil and his angels; agonizing in flame, and refused a drop of water to mitigate the agony. Now, these figures, to the minds both of Jews and Gentiles, must have conveyed a most appalling impression of the misery that was impending over the soul, unless it was relieved from sin and the consequent curse of the law. Jesus knew that the Jews, especially, would understand these figures as implying fearful future punishment. He therefore designed to do what was undoubtedly accomplished in the mind of every one that believed his instruction: which was, to produce a conviction of sin in the soul, by applying to it the requirements of the spiritual law of God, and by showing that the penalty consequent upon sin was fearful and everlasting destruction. We say, then, what every one who has followed these thoughts must perceive to be true, that the instruction of Jesus would necessarily produce, in the mind of every one that *believed*, a conviction that he was a guilty and condemned creature, and that an awful doom awaited his soul unless he received pardon and spiritual deliverance.

Thus, then, by the instruction of Jesus Christ, showing the spirituality and holiness of the divine law, and applying it, with its infinite sanctions, to the exercises of the soul, that condition of mind was produced which alone could prepare man to love a spiritual deliverer; and there is no other way in which the soul could have been prepared, in accordance with truth and the constitution of its own nature, to appreciate the spiritual mercies of God and love him as a spiritual Savior.

The law and the truth being exhibited by Christ in the manner adapted to produce the condition of soul prereqisite to the exercise of affection for spiritual deliverance, now, as God was the author of the law, and as he is the only proper object both of supreme love and obedience, and as man could not be happy in obeying the law without loving its author, it follows that the thing now necessary in order that man's affections might be fixed upon the proper object of love and obedience was, that the supreme God should, by self-denying kindness, manifest spiritual mercy to those who felt their spiritual wants, and thus draw to himself the love and worship of mankind. If any other being should supply the *need*, that being would receive the *love;* it was therefore necessary that *God* HIMSELF should do it, in order that the affection of believers might center upon the proper object.

But notice that, in order to the accomplishment of this end without violating the moral constitution of the universe, it would be essentially necessary that the holiness of God's law should be maintained. This would be necessary, because the law is, in itself, the will of the Godhead, and God himself must be unholy before his will can be. And whatever God may overlook in those who know not their duty, yet when he reveals his perfect law, that law can not, from the nature of its author, allow the commission of a single sin. But besides, if its holiness were not maintained, man is so constituted that *he* could never become holy. Every change to a better course in man's life must be preceded by a conviction of error; man can not repent and turn from sin till he is convicted of sin in himself. Now, if the holiness of the law as a standard of duty was maintained, man might thus be enlightened and convicted of sin, until he has seen and felt the last sin in his soul; and if the law allowed one sin, there would be no way of convicting man of that sin, or of converting him from it. He would therefore remain, in some degree, a sinner forever. But, finally and conclusively, if the holiness of the law was not maintained, that sense of guilt and danger could not be produced which is necessary in order that man may love a spiritual Savior. Jesus produced that condition by applying to the soul the authority, the claims, and the sanctions of the holy law. It is impossible, therefore, in the nature of things, for a sinful being to appreciate God's mercy unless he first feel his justice as manifested in the holy law. Love in the soul is produced by the joint influence of the justice and mercy of God. The integrity of the eternal law, therefore, must be forever maintained.*

---

* The preceding views are confirmed, both by the character of the moral law and by its design and exposition, as given by the apostles of Christ. The moral law, or the rule and obligation of moral rectitude in the sight of God, which is revealed in the Scriptures and interpreted by Christ as obligatory upon the thoughts and feelings of the soul, is not only, in its nature, of perpetual and universal obligation and adapted to produce conviction of sin in every soul that is sensible of transgressing its requirements, but the Scriptures expressly declare that it was designed to produce conviction of sin in the soul, in order to prepare it to receive the gospel.

The moral law is set forth in the Scriptures as holy, just, and good in its character; and whatever may be its effects upon the soul itself, that its character is such no intelligent being in the universe can doubt, because it requires of every one perfect holiness, justice, and goodness; it requires that the soul should be perfectly free from

How, then, could God manifest that mercy to sinners, by which love to himself and to his law would be

sin in the sight of God. And, as we have seen, God ought not to allow one sin; if he did, the law would not be holy, nor adapted to make men holy. But the more holy the law, the more conviction it would produce in the mind of sinners. If the law extended only to external conduct, men would not feel guilty for their wrong thoughts, desires, or designs; and if it extended only to certain classes of spiritual exercises, men would not feel guilty for those which it did not condemn; but, if it required that the soul itself—the spiritual agent, the "I" of the mind—should be holy, and all its thoughts and feelings in accordance with the law of love and righteousness, then the soul would be convicted of guilt for a single wrong exercise, because while it felt that the law was holy, just, and good, it could not but feel condemned in breaking it. When Christ came, therefore, every soul that was taught its spirituality would be convicted of sin. One of two things men had to do: either shut out its light from their soul and refuse to believe its spiritual and perfect requirements, or judge and condemn themselves by those requirements. And while the law thus showed sin to exist in the soul, and condemned the soul as guilty and liable to its penalty, it imparted no strength to the sinner to enable him to fulfill its requirements; it merely sets forth the true standard, which is holy in itself, and which God must maintain, and by its light it shows sinners their guilt, condemns them, and leaves them under its curse.

Now, the Scriptures declare that this is the end which, by its nature, it is adapted to accomplish, and that it was revealed to men with the design to accomplish this end, and thus lead men to see and feel the necessity of justification and pardon by Jesus Christ. The Scripture saith: "It is easier for heaven and earth to pass than one tittle

produced, while his infinite holiness and justice would be obtained?

We answer, in no way possible but by some expedient by which his justice and mercy would both be exalted. If, in the wisdom of the Godhead, such a

of the law to fail;" "The law worketh wrath; where there is no law, there is no transgression;" "Moreover, the law entered that the offense might abound: for where sin abounded, grace did much more abound; that as sin had reigned unto death, even so might grace reign through righteousness, unto eternal life by Jesus Christ our Lord." Mark the following: "Now we know that what things soever the law saith, it saith to them that are under the law; that every mouth may be stopped, and all the world become *guilty* before God; therefore by the deeds of the law shall no flesh be justified: for by the law is the knowledge of sin."

The argument of the apostle in vindicating the holiness of the law, while it, at the same time, produced conviction and condemnation, is conclusive. "What shall we say then? Is the law sin? God forbid. Nay, I had not known sin but by the law: for I had not known lust, except the law had said, Thou shalt not covet [*i. e.*, I would not have felt covetousness to be sin, except the law had condemned it as such]. For I was alive [*i. e.*, not consciously condemned] without the law once: but when the commandment came, sin revived, and I died. And the commandment which was ordained to life [*i. e.*, which required the soul to be holy, and therefore alive to God], I found to be unto death. For sin, taking occasion by the commandment [or acts shown to be sin by the commandment], deceived me, and by it slew me. Wherefore the law is holy, and the commandment is holy, and just, and good. Was then that which is good made death unto me? God forbid. But sin, that it might appear sin [*i. e.*, sin

way could be devised by which God himself could save the soul from the consequences of its guilt; by which he himself could in some way suffer and make self-denials for its good, and, by his own interposition, open a way for the soul to recover from its lost and

which did exist in the soul was made to appear in its true evil character], working death in me by that which is good [*i. e.*, the holiness of the law showed the evil of sin]: that sin by the commandment might become exceedingly sinful. For we know that the law is spiritual: but I am carnal, sold under sin." And then, for deliverance from this bondage he looks to Christ: "For the law of the spirit of life in Christ Jesus hath made me free from the law of sin and death," etc. And mark again: "Is the law then against the promises of God? God forbid; for if there had been a law given that could have given life, verily righteousness would have been of the law [*i. e.*, while the law showed the soul to be unholy and condemned to spiritual death, it provided no means for the relief of the sinner; no influence by which love and holiness could be produced in the heart]. But the Scriptures [that is, the revelation of law in the Scriptures] hath concluded all under sin, that the promise by faith of Jesus Christ might be given to them that believe. But before faith came we were kept under the law, shut up unto the faith which should afterwards be revealed; wherefore the law was our schoolmaster to bring us unto Christ, that we might be justified by faith."

Now, from the above Scriptures, it is evident that the apostle understood the law not only to be adapted, but designed by its author, to show the soul its guilty and lost condition, its inability to free itself from the condemnation to which it was liable, and to prepare it, at the proper time, to trust in and love Christ for salvation from sin, and spiritual death, the consequence of sin.

condemned condition, then the result would follow inevitably that every one of the human family who had been led to see and feel his guilty condition before God, and who believed in God thus manifesting himself to rescue his soul from spiritual death—every one, thus believing, would, from the necessities of his nature, be led to love God his Savior; and—mark—the greater the self-denial and the suffering on the part of the Savior in ransoming the soul, the stronger would be the affection felt for him.

This is the central and vital doctrine of the Plan of Salvation. We will now, by throwing light and accumulating strength upon this doctrine from different points, illustrate and establish it beyond the possibility of rational doubt.

I.

THE TESTIMONY OF JESUS THAT IT WAS NECESSARY MAN SHOULD FEEL THE WANT IN ORDER TO EXERCISE THE LOVE.

Jesus uniformly speaks of it as being necessary that, previously to accepting him as a Savior, the soul should feel the need of salvation. He does not even invite the thoughtless sinner, or the godless worldling, who has no sense of the evil or the guilt of sin, to come to him. Said Jesus: "I came not to call the righteous, but sinners to repentance;" "The whole need not a physician, but they who are sick;" "Come unto me, all ye that labor and are heavy laden, and I will give you rest;" "If any man thirst, let him come unto me and drink;" "Blessed are they that hunger and thirst after righteousness, for they shall be filled." Thus the points which have been shown to be necessary, from the constitution of things, in order to the soul's loving God, are presented in the same light by Jesus himself; and upon the principle which they involve, he acted during his ministry.

II.

THE TESTIMONY OF THE SCRIPTURES THAT GOD DID THUS MANIFEST HIMSELF AS SUFFERING AND MAKING SELF-DENIALS FOR THE SPIRITUAL GOOD OF MEN.

God was in Christ, says the apostle, reconciling the world to himself; that is, God was in Christ doing those things that would restore to himself the obedience and affection of every one that believed. Christ represents himself as a ransom for the soul—as laying down his life for believers. He is represented as descending from an estate of the highest felicity; taking upon him the nature of man, and humbling himself even to the death of the cross—a death of the most excruciating torture—and thus bearing the sins of men in his own body on the tree, that through his death God might be just, and the justifier of every one that believeth in Jesus.

It was thus, by a self-denial surpassing description, by a life of labor for human good, accomplished by constant personal sacrifices, and tending at every step towards the center of the vortex, he went on until, finally, life closed to a crisis by the passion in the garden, the rebuke, and the buffet, and the cruel mockery of the Jews and the Romans; and then, bearing his cross, faint with former agony of spirit, and his flesh quivering with recent scourging, he goes to Calvary, where the agonized sufferer for human sin cried, "IT IS FINISHED," and gave up the ghost.

Such is the testimony of the Scriptures; and it may be affirmed, without hesitancy, that *it would be impossible* for the human soul to exercise full faith in the testimony that it was a guilty and needy creature, condemned by the holy law of a holy God, and that from this condition of spiritual guilt and danger Jesus Christ suffered and died to accomplish its ransom,—we say a human being could not exercise full faith in these truths and not love the Savior.

III.

THE ATONEMENT OF CHRIST PRODUCES THE NECESSARY EFFECT UPON THE HUMAN SOUL, IN RESTORING IT TO AFFECTIONATE OBEDIENCE, WHICH NEITHER PHILOSOPHY, LAW, NOR PRECEPTIVE TRUTH COULD ACCOMPLISH.

The wisdom of Divine Providence was conspicuous in the fact that previously to the introduction of Christianity all the resources of human wisdom had been exhausted in efforts to confer upon man true knowledge and true happiness. Although most of the great names of antiquity were conspicuous rather for those properties which rendered them a terror and a scourge to mankind, and although society among the ancients, in its best estate, was little better than semi-barbarism, yet there was a class in society during the Augustan and 'Periclean age, and even at some periods before that time, that was cultivated in mind and manners. From this class individuals at times arose who were truly great; men distinguished alike for the strength, compass, and discrimination of their intellect. In all the efforts of these men, with the exception of those who applied themselves exclusively to the study of physical phenomena, the great end sought was the means or secret of human happiness. All admitted that human nature, as they found it, was in an imperfect or depraved condition, and not in the enjoyment of its chief good; and the plans which they proposed by which to obtain that happiness of which they believed the soul susceptible, were as various and diverse from each other as can be imagined. No one of these plans ever accomplished, in any degree, the end desired. And no one of them was ever adapted to, or embraced by, the common people. The philosophers themselves, after wrangling for the honor of having discovered truth, and making themselves miserable in the pursuit of happiness. died; and man was left unsatisfied and unhappy, philosophy having shed only sufficient light upon his mind to disclose more fully the guilty and wretched state of his heart.

There are, perhaps, two exceptions to these remarks as applied to the great minds of antiquity: those are Socrates and his pupil Plato. These men, with a far-penetrating insight into the constitutional wants of man, contemplating the disordered and unhappy condition of human nature, and inquiring for a remedy adequate to enlighten the mind and give the heart a satisfying good, perceived that there was not in the resources of philosophy, nor within the compass of human means, any power that could reach the source of the difficulty, and rectify the evil of human nature, which consisted in a want of benevolent affection.* Inferring from the nature of man what would be necessary, and trusting in the goodness of the Deity to grant the requisite aid, they expressed their belief that a divine teacher would come from heaven, who would restore truth and happiness to the human soul.†

It is strange that among philosophers of succeeding ages there has not been wisdom sufficient to discover, from the constitutional necessities of the human spirit, that demand for the instruction and aid of the Mes-

---

* That Plato had some idea of the want, and none of what was necessary to supply it, may be seen in the fact that in order to make men love as brethren, which he saw to be necessary, he recommended a community of wives to the members of his ideal republic.

† In Plato's Dialogue upon the Duties of Religious Worship, a passage occurs, the design of which appears to be to show that man could not, of himself, learn either the nature of the gods or the proper manner of worshiping them, unless an instructor should come from heaven. The following remarkable passage occurs between Socrates and Alcibiades:

"*Socrates.*—To me it appears best to be patient. It is necessary to wait till you learn how you ought to *act* towards the *gods*, and towards *men*.

siah, which Socrates and Plato discovered, even in a comparatively dark age.

There are two insuperable difficulties, which would forever hinder the restoration of mankind to truth and happiness from being accomplished by human means. The first, which has been already alluded to, is, that human instruction, as such, has no power to bind the conscience. Even if man were competent to discover all the truth necessary for a perfect rule of conduct, yet that truth would have no reformatory power, because men could never feel that truth was obligatory which proceeded from merely human sources. It is an obvious principle of our nature that the conscience will not charge guilt on the soul for disobedience, when the command proceeds from a fellow-man, who is not recognized as having the prerogative and the right to require submission. And, besides, as men's minds are variously constituted and of various capacities, there could be no agreement in

---

"*Alcibiades.*—When, O Socrates, shall that time be?, and *who will instruct me?* for most willingly would I see this person, who he is.

"*Socrates.*—He is one who *cares for you;* but, as Homer represents Minerva as taking away darkness from the eyes of Diomedes, that he might *distinguish* a god from a MAN, so it is necessary that he should first take away the darkness from your mind, and then *bring near* those things by which you shall know good and evil.

"*Alcibiades.*—Let him take away the darkness, or any other thing, if he will; for whoever this man is, I am prepared to refuse none of the things which he commands, if I shall be made better."—*Platonis Alcibiad.* ii.

such a case concerning the question, "*What is truth?*" As well might we expect two school-boys to reform each other's manners in school without the aid of the teacher's authority, as that men can reform their fellows without the sanction of that authority which will quicken and bind the conscience. The human conscience was made to recognize and enforce the authority of God, and unless there is belief in the divine obligation of truth, conscience refuses to perform its office.

But the grand difficulty is this: Truth, whether sanctioned by conscience or not, has no power, as has been shown, *to produce love in the heart.* The law may convict and guide the mind, but it has no power to soften or to change the affections. This was the precise thing necessary, and this necessary end the wisdom of the world could not accomplish. All the wisdom of all the philosophers in all ages could never cause the affections of the soul to rise to the holy, blessed God. To destroy selfish pride and produce humility— to eradicate the evil passions, and produce in the soul desires for the universal good, and love for the universal Parent—was beyond the reach of earthly wisdom and power. The wisdom of the world in their efforts to give truth and happiness to the human soul, was foolishness with God; and the wisdom of God— CHRIST CRUCIFIED—was foolishness with the philosophers, in relation to the same subject;* yet it

---

* From an observation of one of the Fathers, it would seem that after the Gospel had been preached among the Greeks many of them perceived its adaptedness to accom-

was divine philosophy: an adapted means, and the only adequate means, to accomplish the necessary end. Said an apostle in speaking upon this subject: "The Jews require a sign, and the Greeks seek after wisdom: but *we preach Christ crucified*, unto the Jews a stumbling-block, and unto the Greeks foolishness; but to them who are called, both Jews and Greeks, *Christ the power of God, and the wisdom of God.*" The Jews, while they required a sign, did not perceive that miracles, in themselves, were not adapted to produce affection. And the Greeks, while they sought after wisdom, did not perceive that all the wisdom of the Gentiles would never work love in the heart. But the apostle preached CHRIST CRUCIFIED, an exhibition of self-denial, of suffering, and of self-sacrificing love and mercy, endured in behalf of men, which, when received by faith, became the power of God and the wisdom of God to produce love and obedience in the human soul. Paul understood the efficacy of the

---

plish the end for which they had sought in vain. "Philosophy," says Clemens of Alexandria, "led the Greeks to Christ, as the law did the Jews."

Concluding paragraph of the apology of M. Minucius Felix in defense of Christianity, A. D. 250: "To conclude: the sum of our boasting is, that we are got into possession of what the philosophers have been always in quest of, and what, with all their application, they could never find. Why, then, so much ill-will stirring against us? If divine truth is come to perfection in our time, let us make a good use of the blessing; let us govern our knowledge with discretion; let superstition and impiety be no more; and let true religion triumph in their stead."

cross. He looked to Calvary and beheld Christ crucified as the sun of the Gospel system. Not as the moon, reflecting cold and borrowed rays; but as the Sun of righteousness, glowing with radiant mercy, and pouring warm beams of life and love into the open bosom of the believer.

IV.

ANALOGY BETWEEN THE MORAL AND PHYSICAL LAWS OF THE UNIVERSE.

The laws which govern physical nature are analogous to those which the Gospel introduces into the spiritual world. The earth is held to the sun by the power of attraction, and performs regularly its circuit around the central, sustaining luminary, maintaining at the same time its equal relations with its sister planets. But the moral system upon the earth is a chaos of derangement. The attraction of *affection*, which holds the soul to God, has been broken, and the soul of man, actuated by selfishness, revolving upon its own center only, jars in its course with its fellow-spirits, and crosses their orbits; and the whole system of the spiritual world upon earth revolves in disorder, the orbs wandering and rolling away from that center of moral life and power which alone could hold them in harmonious and happy motion. Into the midst of this chaos of disordered spirits, God, the Sun of the spiritual world, came down. He shed light upon the moral darkness, and by coming near, like the approaches of a mighty magnet, the attraction of his mercy, as manifested in Christ crucified, became so powerful that many spirits, rolling away into darkness and destruction, felt the efficacy, and were drawn back, and caused to move again, in their regular orbits, around the "Light" and "Life" and "Love" of the spiritual system.

If free agency could be predicated of the bodies of the solar system, the great law which governs their movements might be expressed thus: *Thou shalt attract the sun with all thy might, and thy sister planets as thyself.* The same expression gives the great law of the spiritual world. "Thou shalt love the Lord with all thy soul, and thy neighbor as thyself." Now, if a planet had broken away from its orbit, it would have a tendency to fly off forever, and it never could be restored, unless the sun, the great center of attraction, could, in some way, follow it in its wanderings, and thus by the increased power of his attraction, as he approached nearer to the fallen planet, attach it to himself, and then draw it back again to its original orbit. So with the human spirit: its affections were alienated from God, the center of spiritual attraction, and they could never have been restored, unless God had approached, and by the increased power of his mercy, as manifested in the self-denial, sufferings, and death of Christ, united man again to himself by the power of affection, that he might thus draw him up from his misery and sin, to revolve around him in harmony and love forever.

If this earth had, by some means, broken away

from the sun, there would be no way possible of recovering it again to its place in the system but that which has been mentioned,—that the sun should leave his central position, and approach the wandering orb, and thus, by the increased power of his attraction, draw back the earth to its original position. But the sun could not thus leave the center of the system without drawing all the other planets from their orbits by the movement to recover the lost one. The relations of the system would be broken up, and the whole solar economy sacrificed, if the universal and equal law of gravitation was infringed by the sun changing his position and his relations in the system.

Further: the established laws of the physical universe would render it impossible that any other planet should be the instrument of recovering the earth to the sun. If another planet should approach the earth while thus wandering, the increased power of attraction would cause the two globes to revolve around each other; or if the approaching planet was of greater magnitude, the earth would revolve, as a satellite, around it. But this would not be to restore the earth to its place in the system, nor to its movement around the sun, but to fix it in a wrong position and a wrong movement, and thus alienate it forever from the central source of light and heat. It follows, therefore, that in accordance with the established laws of the solar system, the earth could never be recovered, but would fly off forever, or be broken into asteroids.

There would, therefore, be no way possible for the

recovery of the earth, unless God should adopt an expedient unknown to the physical laws of the universe. (This, all who believe that God is almighty, and himself the author of those laws, will allow that he might do.) That expedient must not destroy the great laws of the system, upon which the safety of all its parts depend, but an augmented force of attraction must be thrown upon the earth from the sun itself, which would be sufficient to check the force of its departing momentum and gradually draw it back to its place. If a portion of the magnetic power of the sun could be thrown into the earth, an adhesion would take place between it and the earth; and then, after the cord was fastened, if that body of attractive matter could ascend again to the body of the sun, the earth would receive the returning impulse, and a new and peculiar influence would be created to draw it back to its allegiance to the sun. If, as has been said, the power came from any other body but the sun itself, or attracted towards any other body, the earth would lose its place in the system forever.*

So in the moral world: God's relations to the moral universe must be sustained. The infinite justice and holiness of the divine law must not be com-

---

* These illustrations are not to be applied to the mode of existence, or subsistence, in the Godhead, but as God is the author of both the physical and moral laws, and as the attraction of gravitation in physics corresponds with the attraction of affection in morals, an analogy of what would be necessary under one is taken to what was accomplished by Christ under the other.

promised. The end to be gained is to draw man, as a revolted sinner, back to God, while the integrity of God's moral government is maintained. Now, *affection* is the attraction of the moral universe; and, in accordance with the foregoing deduction, to reclaim alienated man to God would be impossible, unless there should be a manifestation of the Godhead in the world, to attract to himself man's estranged affections, and then, after the affinity was fastened by faith, by his ascending again to the bosom of the Deity, mankind would thus be gradually drawn back to allegiance to Jehovah.

V.

ILLUSTRATIONS FROM NATURE AND THE SCRIPTURES.

The Plan of Salvation is likened unto a vine which has fallen down from the boughs of an oak. It lies prone upon the ground; it crawls in the dust, and all its tendrils and claspers, which were formed to hold it in the lofty place from which it had fallen, are twined around the weed and the bramble; and having no strength to raise itself, it lies fruitless and corrupting, tied down to the base things of the earth. Now, how shall the vine arise from its fallen condition? But one way is possible for the vine to rise again to the place from whence it had fallen. The bough of the lofty oak must be let down, or some communication must be formed connected with the top of the oak and, at the same time, with the earth. Then, when the bough of the oak was let down to the place where the vine lay, its tender claspers might fasten upon it, and, thus supported, it might raise itself up, and bloom and bear fruit again in the lofty place from whence it fell. So with man: his affections had fallen from God, and were fastened to the base things of the earth. Jesus Christ came down, and by his humanity stood upon the earth, and by his divinity raised his hands and united himself with the Deity of the everlasting Father. Thus the fallen affections of man may fasten upon him, and twine around him, until they again ascend to the bosom of the Godhead from whence they fell.

It was thus that prophets, evangelists, apostles, and the Son of God himself, presented the divine scheme of human redemption. Christ is the "Branch" by which the vine may recover itself from its prone and base condition; he is the "Arm of the Lord," by which he reaches down and rescues sinful men from the ruins of the fall: "through whom," says Peter, "ye believe *in God*"—*i. e.*, believe in God manifested through Christ—"that raised him up from the dead, and gave him glory, that your *faith and hope might be in God.*" Says Paul, "Your life is hid with Christ in God." Jesus himself proclaimed that the believer should have within him "a well of water, springing up into everlasting life;" that is, he that believeth in Christ crucified, the hard heart within him will be struck by the rod of faith, and in his soul there will be a well of pure and living affection, springing up to God forever. And again: "Jesus cried, and said, He that believeth on me, believeth not on me, but on him that sent me; and he that seeth me, seeth him that sent me;" that is, Christ was *God acting*, developing the divine attributes through human nature, so that men might apprehend and realize them. God might have been as merciful as he is if Christ had never died; but man could never have known the extent, nor felt the power, of his mercy, but by the exhibition on the cross. His mercy could have been manifested to man's HEART in no other way. And men can not love God for what he truly is, unless they love him as manifested in the suffering and death of Christ Jesus. "I am the way, the truth, and the life; no man cometh unto the Father, but by me;" "If ye had known me, ye would have known my Father also, and from henceforth ye know him, and have seen him."

VI.

THE PRECEDING VIEWS ESTABLISHED BY REDUCTIO AD ABSURDUM.

It is necessary that man should know the character of the true God, and feel the influence of that character upon his mind and heart. But human nature, as at present constituted, could not be made to feel the goodness of God's mercy, unless God (blessed be his name!) should make self-denials for man's benefit, either by assuming human nature, or in some other way. (*And is it not true that God could make self-denials for men in no other way that would be plain to their apprehension, except by embodying his Godhead in human nature?*) Mercy can be manifested to man, so as to make an impression upon his heart, in no other way than by labor and self-denial. This principle is obvious. Suppose an individual is confined under condemnation of the law, and the governor in the exercise of his powers pardons him: this act of clemency would produce upon the heart of the criminal no particular effect, either to make him grateful or to make him better. He might, perhaps, be sensible of a complacent feeling for the release granted; but so long as he knew that his release cost the governor nothing but a volition of his will, there would be no basis in the prisoner's mind for gratitude and love. The liberated man would feel more gratitude to one of his friends who had labored to get petitions before the governor for his release than he would to the governor who released him.

To vary the illustration: Suppose that two persons who are liable to be destroyed in the flames of a burning dwelling are rescued by two separate individuals. The one is enabled to escape by an individual who, perceiving his danger, steps up to the door and opens it without any effort or self-denial on his part. The other is rescued in a different manner. An individual, perceiving his danger and liability to death, ascends to him, and by a severe effort, and while he is himself suffering from the flames, holds open the door until the inmate escapes for his life. Now, the one who opened the door without self-denial may have been merciful, and the individual relieved would recognize the act as a kindness done to one in peril; but no one would feel that *that* act proved that the man who delivered the other manifested any special mercy, because any man would have done the same act. But the one who ascended the ladder and rescued, by peril and by personal suffering, the individual liable to death, would manifest special mercy, and all who observed it would acknowledge the claim; and the individual rescued would feel the mercy of the act, melting his heart into gratitude to his deliverer, unless his heart was a moral petrifaction.

What are, in reality, the facts by which alone men may know that any being possesses a benevolent nature? Not, certainly, by that being conferring benefits upon others which cost him neither personal labor nor self-denial; because we could not tell but these favors would cease the moment they involved the least degree of sacrifice, or the moment they interfered with his selfish interests. But when it requires a sacrifice on the part of a benefactor to bestow a favor, and that sacrifice is made, then benevolence of heart is made evidently manifest. Now mark: any being who is prompted by benevolence of heart to make sacrifices may not lose happiness, in the aggregate, by so doing, for a benevolent nature finds happiness in performing benevolent acts. *Self-denials are, therefore, not only the appropriate method of manifesting benevolence to men, but they are likewise the appropriate manifestations of a benevolent nature.* Now, suppose

God is perfectly benevolent; then it follows, in view of the foregoing deductions, in order to manifest his true nature to men, self-denials would be necessary in order that men might see and *feel* that "God is love."

It is clear, therefore, that those who reject the divinity of Christ as connected with the atonement, can not believe in God's benevolence, because God is really as benevolent as the self-denials of Christ (believed in as divine) will lead men to feel that he is; nor can they believe in the mercy of God in any way that will produce an effect upon their hearts. To say that the human heart can be deeply affected by mercy that is not manifested by self-denial is to show but little knowledge of the springs which move the inner life of the human soul. Man will feel a degree of love and gratitude for a benefactor who manifests an interest in his wants, and labors to supply them; but he will feel a greater degree of grateful love for the benefactor who manifests an interest in his wants, and makes self-denials to aid him. To deny, therefore, the divine and meritorious character of the atonement is to shut out both the evidence and the effect of God's mercy from the soul.

In accordance with this view is the teaching of the Scriptures. There is but one thing which is charged against men in the New Testament as a fundamental and soul-destroying *heresy*, and that is not denying the Lord, but "denying the Lord that *bought* them." It is rejecting the purchase of Christ by his self-denying atonement which causes the destruction of the soul, because it rejects the truth which alone can produce love to the God of love.

But further: the facts have been fully proved that God Jehovah, by taking a personal interest in the well-being of the Israelites and laboring to secure their redemption, secured their affections to himself; and that his acts of mercy produced this effect was manifested by their song after their final deliverance at the Red Sea: "O sing unto Jehovah, for he has triumphed gloriously; the horse and his rider he has thrown into the sea. Jehovah is my strength and song, and has become my salvation." In like manner Jesus Christ secured to himself, in a greater degree, the affections of Christians, by his self-denying life and death, to ransom them from *spiritual* bondage and misery. The Israelites in Egypt were under a *temporal* law so severe that, while they suffered in the greatest degree, they could not fulfill its requirements; they therefore loved Jehovah for *temporal* deliverance. The believer was under a *spiritual* law, the requirements of which he could not fulfill, and therefore he loved Christ for *spiritual* deliverance. This fact, that the supreme affection of believers was thus fixed upon Christ, and fixed upon him in view of his self-sacrificing love for them, is manifest throughout the whole New Testament—even more manifest than that the Jews loved Jehovah for temporal deliverance. "The love of Christ constrains me," says one: thus manifesting that his very life was actuated by affection for Jesus.

Says another, speaking of early Christians generally, "Whom [Christ] having not seen, *ye love*; and in whom, though now you see him not, yet believing, ye rejoice with joy unspeakable and full of glory." The Bible requires men to perform their religious duties, moved by love to Christ: "And whatsoever ye do, do it heartily, as to the Lord, and not unto men: knowing that of the Lord ye shall receive the reward of the inheritance: for ye serve the Lord Christ." Mark: these Christians were moved in what they *did*, what they *said*, and what they *felt*, by love to Christ. Love to Jesus actuated their whole being, body, and soul; it governed them.

Now, suppose that Jesus Christ was not God, nor a true manifestation of the Godhead in human nature, but a man, or angel, authorized by God to accomplish the redemption of the human race from sin and misery. In doing this, it appears, from the nature of things and from the Scriptures, that he did what was adapted to, and what *does*, draw the heart of every true believer—as in the case of the apostle and the early Christians—unto himself, as the supreme or governing object of affection. Their will is governed by the will of Christ; and love to him moves their heart and hands. Now, if it be true that Jesus Christ is not God, then he has devised and executed a plan by which the supreme affections of the human heart are drawn to himself, and alienated from God, the proper object of love and worship; and God having authorized this plan, he has devised means to make man love Christ, the creature, more than the Creator, who is God over all, blessed for evermore.

But is it said that, Christ having taught and suffered by the will and authority of God, we are under obligation to love God for what Christ has done for us? It is answered that this is impossible. We can not love one being for what another does or suffers in our behalf. We can love no being for labors and self-denials in our behalf but that being who voluntarily labors and denies himself. *It is the kindness and mercy exhibited in the self-denial that moves the affections;* and the affections can move to no being but the one that makes the self-denials, because it is the self-denials that draw out the love of the heart.

Is it still said that Christ was sent by God to do his will, and not his own; and therefore we ought to love God, as the being to whom gratitude and love is due for what Christ said and suffered? Then it is answered: If God willed that Christ, as a creature of his, should come, and by his sufferings and death redeem sinners, we ought not to love Christ for it, because he did it as a creature, in obedience to the commands of God, and was not self-moved nor meritorious in the work; and we can not love God for it, for the labor and the self-denial were not borne by him.

And further, if one being, by an act of his authority, should cause another innocent being to suffer in order that he might be loved who had imposed the suffering but not borne it, it would render him unworthy of love. If God had caused Jesus Christ, being his creature, to suffer that he might be loved himself for Christ's sufferings, while he had no connection with them, instead of such an exhibition on the part of God producing love to him, it would produce pity for Christ, and aversion towards God. So that neither God nor Christ, nor any other being, can be loved for mercy extended by self-denials to the needy, unless those self-denials were produced by a voluntary act of mercy upon the part of the being who suffers them. And no being but the one who made the sacrifices could be meritorious in the case. It follows, therefore, uncontrovertibly, that if Christ was a creature— no matter of how exalted worth—and not God, and if God approved of his work in saving sinners, he approved of treason against his own government: because, in that case, the work of Christ was adapted to draw, and did necessarily draw, the affections of the human soul to himself as its spiritual Savior, and thus alienate them from God, their rightful object. And Jesus Christ himself had the design of drawing men's affections to himself in view by his crucifixion. Says he, "And I, if I be lifted up from the earth, will draw all men unto me." This he said, signifying what death he should die: thus distinctly stating that it was the self-denials and mercy exhibited in the crucifixion that would draw out the affections of the human soul, and that those affections would be drawn to himself as the suffering Savior. But that God would sanction a scheme which would involve treason against himself, and that Christ should participate in it, is absurd and impossible, and therefore can not be true.

But if the divine nature was united with the human, in the teaching and work of Christ; if "God was in Christ," drawing the affections of men, or "reconciling the world to himself;" if, when Christ was lifted up, as Moses lifted up the serpent in the wilderness, he drew, as he said he would, the affections of all believers to himself; and then if he ascended, as the second person of the Trinity, into the bosom of the eternal Godhead,—he thereby, after he had engaged, by his work on earth, the affections of the human soul, bore them up to the bosom of the Father, from whence they had fallen. Thus the ruins of the fall were rebuilt, and the affections of the human soul again restored to God, the Creator and proper object of supreme love. O, the length and the breadth, and the depth and the height of the divine wisdom and goodness, as manifested in the wonderful Plan of Salvation! "Great is the mystery of godliness. God was manifest in the flesh, justified in the spirit, seen of angels, preached unto the Gentiles, believed on in the world, received up into glory." Amen. Blessing and honor, dominion and power, be unto him that sitteth upon the throne, and unto the Lamb, for ever and ever! Amen and amen.

Chapter XVI.

CONCERNING THE INFLUENCE OF FAITH IN CHRIST UPON THE MORAL DISPOSITION AND MORAL POWERS OF THE SOUL.

It has been demonstrated that the teaching and atonement of God the Savior would draw to him, by faith, the affections of the human heart. We will now inquire what particular effect that faith in Christ, which works by love, has upon the moral disposition, the conscience, the imagination, and the life of believers. Would faith in Christ, as a divine, suffering Savior, quicken and regulate and harmonize the moral powers of the soul?

I.

THE INFLUENCE OF FAITH IN CHRIST UPON THE MORAL DISPOSITION OF THE SOUL.

When its disposition is affected, the soul is affected to the center of its being. By disposition is meant the desires or predilections of the heart, which influence the choice of the will to good or evil. The radical difference of character in spirits depends upon their disposition. The spirit that has a settled love for sin and hatred for holiness is a devil, whether it be in time or eternity, embodied or disembodied. And that spirit which has a settled love for holiness is a benevolent spirit, in whatever condition it exists. A devil, or malignant spirit, is one that seeks its gratification in habitually doing evil. A holy being, or benevolent spirit, is one that finds its gratification in habitually doing good. Whatever, therefore, affects the moral disposition of the soul, affects radically the character of the soul. It becomes, therefore, a question of the deepest interest: What effect will faith in Christ have upon man's moral disposition?

The solution of this inquiry is not difficult. *Is Jesus Christ holy?* All Christendom, skeptics and believers, answer in the affirmative. Now, the love of a holy being will, as a necessary result, conteract unholiness in the heart. Holiness is the antagonist principle of sin. The soul can not love a holy being, and at the same time cherish those principles and exercises which it is conscious are offensive to the soul of the beloved object. From the nature of the case, love to holiness will produce opposition to sin. Love is the fulfilling of the law, and sin is the transgression of the law; so that, while the soul is entirely actuated in all its exercises by pure love to Christ, those exercises of the heart can not be sinful.

When the heart is attached to any being, especially when that being is lovely and pure in his character, it becomes averse to every thing which, from its evil nature, causes suffering to the object of its affections. There are few things which will cause one to feel so sensibly the evil of sin as to see that his sins are causing anguish to one that he loves.

It is said of Zeleucus, a king of the ancient Locri, that he enacted a law the penalty of which was that the offender should lose both his eyes. One of his sons became a transgressor of that law. The father had his attachment to his son, and the law he himself had promulgated as righteous in its requirements and in its penalty. The lawgiver, it is said, ordered his son into his presence, and required that one of his eyes should be taken out; and then, in order to show mercy to his son, and at the same time maintain the penalty of the law, he sacrificed one of his own eyes as a ransom for the remaining eye of his child. Now, we do not refer to this case as a perfect analogy, but to show the moral effect of such an exhibition of justice and self-sacrificing mercy. As man is constituted, it is perfectly certain that this transaction would produce two effects: one upon the subjects of the king, which would be to impress upon every heart that the law was sacred, and that the lawgiver thus regarded it. This impression would be made much more strongly than it would have been if the king had ordered that his son should lose both his eyes; because it manifested, in the strongest manner possible, his love for his son and his sacred regard for his law. If he had allowed his son to escape, it would have exhibited to his subjects less love for his law, and if he had executed the whole penalty of the law upon the son, instead of bearing a portion of it himself, he would have manifested less love for his son. The king was the lawgiver; he therefore had the power to pardon his son, without inflicting the penalty upon him, and without enduring any sacrifice himself. Every mind, therefore, would feel that it was a voluntary act on the part of the king; and such an exhibition of justice and mercy, maintaining the law and saving his son by his own sacrifice, would impress all minds with the deepest reverence for the character of the lawgiver and for the sacredness of the law.

But another effect, deep and lasting in its character, would be produced upon the son who had transgressed the law. Every time that he looked upon his father, or remembered what he had suffered for his transgression, it would increase his love for him, increase his reverence for the law, and cause an abhorrence of his crime to arise in his soul. His feelings would be more kind towards his sire, more submissive to the law, and more averse to transgression.

Now, this is precisely the effect necessary to be produced in order that pardon may be extended to transgressors, and yet just and righteous government be maintained. If civil law had some expedient by which, with the offer of pardon, some influence could be exerted upon the heart of the transgressor which would entirely change his character, an influence which would make him love the law he had transgressed, hate the crime he had committed, hate himself for committing it, and implant within him the spirit of an obedient and faithful subject—if such an effect could be produced by pardon, then pardon would be safe; because there would be some means, or some moral power connected with it, that would, at the same time that the pardon was granted, change the moral disposition of the criminal from that of a rebellious to that of a faithful and affectionate subject. This expedient the civil law can never have. Such an expedient was that of Zeleucus, the self-sacrificed lawgiver and father. Such an expedient, in some respects, in the moral government of God, is the atoning sacrifice of Jesus Christ. "Christ," says the prophet, "was bruised for our iniquities;" says the apostle, "He bore our sins in his own body on the tree;" says himself, "This is my body, *broken for you.*" Now, two effects would follow this exhibition of the self-sacrificing love of Christ. One in the heart of the believing sinner: every time he realized by faith that the divine Savior suffered the rebuke, the scorn, and the cross, as a sacrifice for his sins, he would regard the Savior with greater love; and sin, which caused the suffering of his divine Benefactor, he would regard in himself and others with greater abhorrence. Another effect which would result would be, that all the holy beings in the universe, if they had knowledge of the self-sacrifice of God the Savior as an atonement to maintain the law and redeem sinners, would be inspired with greater reverence for the eternal law, and greater aversion to sin. Thus would the faith of Christ affect the moral disposition of believers, and of all holy beings throughout the universe; drawing the believer back to holiness and obedience, and adding a new motive to confirm holy beings in happy allegiance.

The language of the apostle confirms this view: "What the law could not do, in that it was weak through the flesh, God, sending his own Son in the likeness of sinful flesh, and for sin, condemned sin in the flesh;" that is, the law, although it had power to show to the mind the evil and the guilt of sin, had no power to produce in the heart an aversion to it; but Christ, coming in the body and dying for sin; in that way reaches man's moral feelings, and creates a sentiment of condemnation of, or aversion to, sin in the heart of every believer.

A feeling cannot be manifested by intellect or will. A communication of knowledge, or law, does not manifest feeling so that it produces feeling in others. The moral feelings of God were manifested by the sacrifice of Christ; and that manifestation, through the flesh, affects the moral feelings of man, assimilates them to God, and produces an aversion to sin, the abominable thing which God hates. Blessed faith! which, while it purifies the heart, works by the sweet influence of love in accomplishing the believer's sanctification.

II.

THE INFLUENCE OF FAITH IN CHRIST UPON THE MORAL SENSE OR CONSCIENCE OF BELIEVERS.

To a mind endowed with the higher qualities of reason there can be no more interesting thought than that noticed in a previous demonstration; which was, that a man's conscience is guided by his faith. Conscience is the highest moral faculty, or rather the governing moral power of the soul, and this governing faculty is regulated and controlled by faith. Man's conscience always follows his religious belief, and changes with it, and grows weak or strong with it.

Now, God has so constituted the soul that the affections, and likewise the conscience, are affected and controlled by faith, and the purity of the one and the integrity of the other, and the activity of both, depend upon what man believes; this being true, no mind can avoid the conviction that the principle of FAITH, which Christ has laid at the foundation of the Christian system is, from the nature of things, the only principle through the operation of which man's moral powers can be brought into happy, harmonious, and perfect activity. But this happy effect, as has been shown, can be produced only by faith in the Truth; and, besides, it is an intuition of reason that God certainly would not make the soul so that its moral powers would be controlled by faith, and then cause that faith in falsehood should perfect and make happy those powers. Such a supposition would be a violation of reason, as well as an impiety. In searching, therefore, for the answer to the inquiry, *What is Truth?* as it concerns the spiritual interests of man, the direct process of solution would be to inquire what effect certain facts, or supposed facts, would have upon the moral disposition and moral powers of the soul; and that faith which quickens and rectifies those powers, as we have noticed, is necessarily truth.

We come now to the inquiry, *What effect has faith in Christ—in the divinity of his person, in his teaching, and in his atonement for sin—upon the conscience of believers?*

The answer is plain. Those who received Christ as possessing supreme authority as a divine teacher— their faith would so affect their conscience that it would reprove for every neglect of conformity to the example of Jesus. The moment faith recognizes Christ as a divine instructor, that moment conscience recognizes his instruction and his example as obligatory to be received and practiced. To the believer the teachings and example of Christ have not only the force of truth, recognized as such by the understanding, but they have likewise the authority of supreme law, as coming from that Divine Being who is the rightful lawgiver of the soul. Now, then, if faith in Christ would regulate the conscience according to his example and precepts, the only inquiry which remains is, Were the example and precepts of Christ a perfect rule of duty towards God and men? This inquiry has been the subject of examination in another chapter, in which the fact was shown—which has been generally admitted by all men, believers and skeptics—that Christ's example of piety towards God and kindness towards men was perfect. When this is admitted, the consecutive fact follows, whether men perceive it or not, that in the case of all who receive him as their Lord and lawgiver, the conscience would be regulated according to a perfect standard, and guided by a perfect rule.

But further: While it is true that a knowledge of duty guides the conscience, and a knowledge of the divine authority of the lawgiver binds it by imposing a sense of obligation, it is likewise true that faith in Christ's atoning sacrifice has peculiar efficacy to strengthen this sense of obligation. Two men may have an equal knowledge of duty, and yet one feel, much more than the other, a sense of obligation to perform it: whatever, therefore, increases the sense of obligation increases the power of conscience, and thereby promotes in a greater degree active conformity of the life to the rule of duty.

The atonement of Christ increases the sense of obligation by waking into exercise gratitude and hope in the soul of the believer. Gratitude gives the conscience a power in the soul where it exists, which could arise from no other source. Conscience reproves for the neglect of known duty; but to neglect duty, when it involves the sense of gratitude to the kindest of benefactors, is to arm the moral sense of the soul with a two-edged sword. When the lawgiver is likewise the benefactor, conscience rebukes, not only for wrong doing, but for ingratitude.

One step further: When the being who claims our obedience is not only our benefactor, but the object of all our hopes, the power of obligation is still further increased. To disobey a being whom we ought to obey would be wrong; to disobey that being if he was our self-denying benefactor would be ingratitude added to the wrong; and to disobey that being if from him we hoped for all future good would be to add unworthiness to wrong and ingratitude. Thus faith in Christ Jesus combines the sense of wrong, of ingratitude, and unworthiness, in the rebuke which conscience gives to the delinquent believer; and obedience to the Redeemer's example and precepts is enforced by the united power of duty, gratitude, and hope.

Further, and finally: Conscience recognizes the fact that our obligation to gratitude is in proportion to the benefit conferred. If a benefactor has endured great sacrifices and self-denials to benefit us, the obligation of gratitude binds us the more strongly to respect the will and feelings of that individual. Conscience feels the obligation of gratitude just in proportion to the self-denials and sacrifices made in our behalf. If a friend risks his interest to the amount of a dollar or an hour of time to benefit us, the obligation of gratitude upon the conscience is light, but still there is a sense of obligation; but if a friend risks his life, and wades through deep afflictions to confer benefits, the universal conscience of man would affirm the obligation, and would reprobate the conduct of the individual benefited as base and unnatural if he did not ever after manifest an affectionate regard for the interests and the desires of his benefactor.

Thus by faith in Jesus Christ the conscience is not only guided by a perfect rule, but it is likewise quickened and empowered by a perfect sense of obligation. Christ is the divine lawgiver; therefore it is right to obey him. He is our benefactor; gratitude, therefore, requires obedience. But, as our benefactor, he has endured the utmost self-denial and sacrifice for our sake; therefore we are under the utmost obligation of gratitude to return self-denial and sacrifice for his sake. Or, in the words of an apostle, "He died for all, that they which live should not henceforth live unto themselves, but unto him who died for them, and rose again;" and, added to this, our hope of all future good rests in the same Being that right and gratitude require us to obey and love. Thus does a perfect faith in Christ perfect the conscience of believers, by guiding, quickening, and by producing a perfect sense of obligation.

III.

THE INFLUENCE OF FAITH IN CHRIST UPON THE IMAGINATION.

There are few exercises of the mind fraught with so much evil, and yet so little regarded, as that of an evil imagination. Many individuals spend much of their time in a labor of spirit which is vain and useless, and often very hurtful to the moral character of the soul. The spirit is borne off upon the wings of an active imagination, and expatiates among ideal conceptions that are improbable, absurd, and sinful. Some people spend about as much time in day-dreams as they do in night-dreams. Imaginations of popularity, pleasure, or wealth, employ the minds of worldly men; and perchance the Christian dreams of wealth and of magnificent plans of benevolence, or of schemes less pious in their character. It is difficult to convey a distinct idea of the evil under consideration, without supposing a case like the following:

One day, while a young man was employed silently about his usual pursuits, he imagined a train of circumstances by which he supposed himself to be put in possession of great wealth; and then he imagined that he would be the master of a splendid mansion, surrounded with grounds devoted to profit and amusement; he would keep horses and conveyances that would be perfect in all points, and servants that would want nothing in faithfulness or affection; he would be great in the eyes of men, and associate with the great among men, and render himself admired or honored by his generation. Thus his soul wandered for hours amid the ideal creations of his own fancy.

Now, much of men's time, when their attention might be employed by useful topics of thought, is thus spent in building "castles in the air." Some extraordinary circumstance is thought of by which they might be enriched, and then hours are wasted in foolishly imagining the manner in which they would expend their imaginary funds. Such excursions of the fancy may be said to be comparatively innocent; and they are so, compared with the more guilty exercises of a great portion of mankind. The mind of the politician and the partisan divine is employed in forming schemes of triumph over their opponents. The minds of the votaries of fashion, of both sexes, are employed in imagining displays and triumphs at home and abroad; and those of them who are vicious at heart, not having their attention engaged by any useful occupation, pollute their souls by cherishing imaginary scenes of folly and lewdness. And not only the worthless votaries of the world, but likewise the followers of the holy Jesus, are sometimes led captive by an unsanctified imagination. Not that they indulge in the sinful reveries which characterize the unregenerate sons and daughters of time and sense; but their thoughts wander to unprofitable topics, and wander at times when they should be fixed on those truths which have a sanctifying efficacy upon the heart. In the solemn assemblies for public worship, many of those whose bodies are bowed and their eyes closed in token of reverence for God are yet mocking their Maker by assuming the external semblance of worshipers, while their souls are away wandering amid a labyrinth of irrelevant and sinful thought.

It is not affirmed that the exercises of the imagination are necessarily evil. Imagination is one of the noblest attributes of the human spirit; and there is something in the fact that the soul has power to create, by its own combinations, scenes of rare beauty and of perfect happiness, unsullied by the imperfections which pertain to earthly things, that indicates not only its nobility, but perhaps its future life. When the imagination is employed in painting the beauties of nature, or in collecting the beauties of sentiment and devotion, and in grouping them together by the sweet measures of poetry, its exercises have a benign influence upon the spirit. It is like presenting "apples of gold in pictures of silver" for the survey of the soul. The imagination may degrade and corrupt, or it may elevate and refine, the feelings of the heart. The inquiry, then, is important, How may the exercises of the imagination be controlled and directed so that their influence upon the soul shall not be injurious, but ennobling and purifying? Would faith in Christ turn the sympathies of the soul away from those gifted but guilty minds,

> "Whose poisoned song
> Would blend the bounds of right and wrong;
> And hold, with sweet but cursed art,
> Their incantations o'er the heart,
> Till every pulse of pure desire
> Throbs with the glow of passion's fire,
> And love, and reason's mild control,
> Yield to the simoom of the soul?"

When the conscience had become purified and quickened, it would be a check upon the erratic movements of the imagination; and when the disposition was corrected, it would be disinclined to every unholy exercise; so that, in the believer, the disinclination of the will and the disapprobation of the conscience would be powerful aids in bringing into subjection the imaginative faculty. But, more than this, faith in Christ would have a direct influence in correcting the evils of the imagination. It is a law of mind that the subject which interests an individual most, subordinates all other subjects to itself, or removes them from the mind and assumes their place. As a group of persons, who might be socially conversing upon a variety of topics, if some venerable individual should enter and introduce an absorbing subject, in which all felt interested, minor topics would be forgotten in the interest created by the master subject: so when "Christ crucified" enters the presence-chamber of the believer's soul, the high moral powers of the mind bow around in obeisance, and even imagination folds her starry wings around her face, and bows before Immanuel. When the cross of Christ becomes the central subject of the soul, it has power to chasten the imagination and subdue its waywardness by the sublime exhibition of the bleeding mercy in the atonement. The apostle perceived the efficacy of the cross in subduing vain reasoning and an evil imagination, and alludes to it in language possessing both strength and beauty, as "casting down imaginations, and every high thing that exalteth itself against the knowledge of God, and (mark) bringing into *captivity* every *thought* to the OBEDIENCE of Christ."

That these views are not idle speculations, but truthful realities, is affirmed by the experience of every Christian. When the imagination is wandering to unprofitable or forbidden subjects, all that is necessary in order to break the chain of evil suggestion, and introduce into the mind a profitable train of thought, is to turn the eye of the soul upon the

"Lamb of God that taketh away the sin of the world." By the presence of this delightful and sacred idea every unworthy and hurtful thought will be awed out of the mind.

Thus does faith in the blessed Jesus control and purify the imagination of believers.

IV.

THE INFLUENCE OF FAITH IN CHRIST UPON THE LIFE, LEADING MAN TO SUCH CONDUCT AS WILL EVENTUALLY ACCOMPLISH HIS SALVATION.

It is certain that men have all the faculties which, if rightly directed, would be necessary to enable them to benefit and bless each other. Suppose one individual did all in his power to do others good and make them happy, who can limit the amount of consolation which that man might impart to the children of want and sorrow, or the amount of light he might shed upon the minds of the ignorant, or the rebukes and warnings he might sound in the ears of those who persisted in sin? Suppose a whole community of such individuals, denying themselves the selfish ease and worldly pleasures which the children of this world seek after, and devoting their lives to spread around them the blessings and benefits of the Gospel—should individuals or communities desire thus to devote their lives to benevolence instead of selfish effort—it is certain the Creator has endowed them with every faculty necessary to the accomplishment of such a work.

They have hearts to love their fellow-men; they have reason and language to learn themselves, and then to instruct others. They can travel to where the ignorant and the needy dwell, either at home or abroad; or, if they feel disqualified personally to do this, they have hands to labor for the means to send others on errands of benevolence throughout the world. That men have been created with the faculties, therefore, to diffuse the blessings which they possess, throughout the world, no one can doubt.

But, second, men are so constituted that the exercise of these faculties in a manner that would bless others would likewise produce a blessing in their own souls. It is a fact in experience as well as philosophy that the exercise of any power of the soul gives increased strength to that power. By exercising their selfish and malevolent feelings men become continually more selfish and malevolent, while, on the contrary, by exercising self-denial and the benevolent feelings men become continually more benevolent. *Selfishness, all admit, is an evil in the heart. Self-denial is its antagonist principle; and it is by invigorating the latter by exercise that the former evil principle is to be eradicated.* It would, therefore, be the greatest benefit to those who possessed blessings to induce them to exercise benevolence by communicating them to others.

It follows, therefore, that not only the greatest good of the guilty and the ignorant requires self-denying benevolence in those who have the means and the power to enlighten and guide them to truth and happiness, but likewise that the greatest good of those possessing blessings is to impart them to others. "It is more blessed to give than to receive," because, by the exercise of self-denial to do good, benevolence is strengthened in the soul; and from benevolent exercises arises the blessedness of the spirit. Men are constantly making sacrifices to advance their own aggrandizement, and thus, by increasing their own selfishness, they make themselves more miserable. The great end to be gained is to lead them to make sacrifices for others, and thus, with others, bless themselves.

Now, no one doubts that the whole human family in the days of Christ needed the blessing of an enlightening and purifying religion. And no one doubts that the ultimate end of a religion from heaven would be the greatest ultimate good of the entire race. Three things, then, are obvious: 1. That a religion from heaven would be designed ultimately to bless the whole world; 2. That the best good of mankind, as a family, required that they should be the instruments in disseminating this religion among themselves; 3. That the principle of self-denial, or denying ourself the ease and pleasures of selfishness in order to perform acts of benevolence, is the great principle by which the operation of spreading this religion would be carried on.

Now, Jesus Christ professed to give a universal spiritual religion, one which encircled in its design, and was to bless by its influence, the whole family of man, and faith he set forth as the great motive-power of the whole plan. The question then is: Would faith in Christ lead men to that method of living and acting, and to the possession of those views and feelings which would make them instrumental in benefiting each other, and which would destroy selfishness and promote the happiness and interest of the whole family of man, in accordance with the three principles above specified?

1. It has been shown that the example and precepts of Christ become the guide to conscience, and the rule of faith and practice for all believers. What, then, has Christ said and done to induce men to do each other good, and to unite the race of man in one harmonious and happy family?

The Gospel of Christ possesses all the characteristics of a universal religion. *It is adapted to human nature; not to any particular country or class of men, but, as has been shown, to the* NATURE *of the race.* Its truths are intelligible, and may be understood by all men, and transferred into all languages. It is spiritual in its character, designed to affect the mind and heart of man; so that wherever intelligent beings are to be found, there it may be introduced into the heart by faith,to correct the spiritual evils of their nature, and produce happiness in the soul.*

The precepts and teaching of Jesus are designed and adapted to harmonize the race of man into one happy family. Instead of the abominations and folly of polytheism, he presented before the minds of men

---
* See Reinhard's Plan, sec. 17, 22.

one common object of worship; and so exhibited the character of that object, by presenting before the world a grand spectacle of self-denying mercy, that the exhibition was *adapted* to attract the attention of all and draw all hearts to one center of affection.

In all his instructions to regulate the conduct of men, he viewed them as brethren of the same great family, and taught them to consider themselves as such. No retaliation was to be offered for injuries received, but the injured child was to appeal only to the Great Parent of the family. No one might treat another as his enemy, and no one was to cease in efforts to do good to another, unless he perceived that those efforts were treated with contempt, and instead of benefiting had a hardening effect upon the heart.

2. Their lives were to be spent in efforts to impart those blessings which they possessed to their brethren of the human family who possessed them not. Instead of the unhallowed and anxious struggle which worldly men manifest to raise themselves to power over their fellows, their efforts were to be directed to the opposite end—to raise the ignorant and the needy to the enjoyment of the blessings and privileges which they possessed.

This active and constant effort to extend the blessings which they possessed to others, and to relieve men from their vices and ignorance, was not to stop with their own kindred or nation or tongue, nor to be restricted to the grateful or the deserving; in this respect their philanthropy was to be modeled after that of their Heavenly Father, who causeth his sun to shine upon the just and the unjust. It was to continue during life, and to extend to the ends of the earth. And in proportion as men were found in a condition of ignorance and want, in the same proportion they were to make benevolent exertions to elevate and bless them.

Now, every one can see that if these precepts were obeyed, strife between individuals and nations would cease, and the glorious process of benevolent effort would go on, until the last benighted mind was enlightened and the last corrupted heart purified by the power of the faith of Christ.

It was necessary, in connection with these precepts, that some motive should be presented to cause men to deny themselves in order to act in accordance with them. Now, it has been shown that the believer acts in view of the character and will of Jesus. Christ, therefore, in order to give these precepts moving power upon the souls of men, identified himself with his needy creatures, and sanctioned the duty which he prescribed to others by conformity to it himself; so that these precepts, given to govern men's conduct in this life, he made the rule of judgment in heaven's court of equity, and by them the decision will be made out, which will settle, finally, the spiritual destiny of men. "Inasmuch as ye did it not to one of the least of these my brethren, ye did it not unto me." Thus Christ identifies himself with the most needy of mankind, and receives an act of kindness done to them as done to himself. When the love of Christ, therefore, constrains men, he has so exhibited his will that it constrains them to act for the good of each other. Those that love Jesus, therefore, and expect his favor, must serve him by doing good to others.

Moreover, Christ has sanctioned these precepts by his own example. His life was a life of self-denying labor for the benefit of our race; and his command to every one is: Deny thyself; take up thy cross, and follow me. Thus, by Christ's precepts, by his example, and especially by his identifying himself with those in need, that method of life is sanctioned which alone could make man the benefactor of his fellows, unite the human family in one happy brotherhood, and make them blessed in doing each other good, in the faith of Christ.

Those that love Jesus will desire to do his will, will find their happiness in obeying him; and that will is, that they should labor to benefit his creatures. Those who believe in and love Jesus will have their conscience regulated by his precepts and example. Thus the conscience of believers is set, if I may so express it, so that it will regulate the movement of their life.

It follows, therefore, that faith in Jesus Christ is directly designed and adapted to strengthen men's benevolent affections, and to produce in believers that active desire and effort for the good of others which will necessarily produce the dissemination of the light and love of the Gospel throughout the habitable world.

Chapter XVII.

CONCERNING THE DESIGN AND THE IMPORTANCE OF THE MEANS OF GRACE.

I.—Prayer.

It has been shown that, constituted as we are, the manifestations made of the character and attributes of God in the Scriptures are adapted to produce the greatest good in the human spirit; and in order that that good may be effected it is necessary that the truths of the Scripture be brought into contact with the soul, that it may be impressed and influenced by them. The truths and manifestations of Revelation are the elements of moral power, which, apprehended by faith, are effective in purifying the fountain of life in the soul, and in rectifying and regulating its exercises; it follows, therefore, that the requirement to bring those truths before the mind in a particular manner would be a duty necessarily connected with the revelation of the doctrines, as directions for taking the medicine are connected with the prescription of a physician into whose hands a patient has submitted himself. Now, prayer, or worship, is one method by which the truths and manifestations of Revelation are directly brought before the contemplation of the soul. Prayer brings the mind to the immediate contemplation of God's character, and holds it there, till by comparison and aspiration the believer's soul is properly impressed, and his wants properly felt. The more subtle physical processes and affinities become, the better are the analogies which they furnish of processes in the spiritual world. The influence of believing prayer has a good analogy in the modern invention of the photograph. By means of this process the features of natural objects are thrown upon a sensitive sheet through a lens, and leave their impression upon that sheet. So when the character of God is, by means of prayer, brought to bear upon the mind of the believer—that mind being rendered sensitive by the Holy Spirit—it impresses there the divine image. In this manner the image of Christ is formed in the soul, the existence of which the Scriptures represent as inspiring the believer with the hope of glory.

In the introductory chapter it is shown that the impulse which leads men to worship proves a curse to the soul, where the objects worshiped are unholy, and that the only remedy for the evil is the revelation of a holy object for the supreme homage of the human soul. So soon as a righteous and benevolent God is presented before the mind, then prayer becomes a blessing instead of a curse to the soul. Look at the subject in the form of a syllogism :

Man, by worshiping, becomes assimilated to the moral character of the object that he worships :

The God of the Bible, as manifest in Christ Jesus, is the only perfectly righteous and perfectly benevolent Being ever worshiped by man :

Therefore, man can become righteous and benevolent in no other way than by that worship which will assimilate him to the God of the Bible.

And, further, as it has been demonstrated that righteousness and benevolence produce the rectitude and the happiness—the greatest good—of the soul, man can gain the great end of his being only by that worship which assimilates his nature to the moral image of God.

It follows, therefore, that prayer is a necessary and most important means of grace—a duty growing out of the nature of the case, and a duty upon which depends, in a great measure, the well-being of the human spirit. The apostle understood the philosophy of this subject when he said, " But we all, with open face, beholding as in a glass the glory of the Lord, are changed into the same image, from glory to glory, even as by the Spirit of the Lord." Therefore it is that the commandment that men should pray is presented in the Bible in every variety of language; and it is constantly repeated by the inspired writers and by the Son of God himself, who commended, by his precepts and example, private, social, and public prayer, and who taught by a parable that "men ought always to pray and not to faint."

The Importance of Strong Desire and Importunity in Prayer.

It is impossible to produce grateful feelings by granting a benefit for which the recipient has no desire. If a child asked for bread when it was not hungry, and if, while the child had no feeling of want, its *un*felt request was answered by its father, it could neither appreciate the gift nor be grateful for it. The soul is so constituted, as has been fully shown, that it must really feel the need of the benefit before it can appreciate its importance, or be grateful for the favor received. So it is in the case of the suppliant in prayer: if he has an anxious desire, a spirit of importunate solicitude, for the blessing which he asks, when he receives it, gratitude and praise will, as the consequence of gratified desire, spring up in the heart. Now mark: if there was not a feeling of importunate desire in the mind of the suppliant, God could not be glorified nor the creature benefited by an answer to prayer. God could not be glorified, because his goodness would not be felt and acknowledged in the answer; and the creature could not be benefited, because it is the feeling of gratitude and praise in his own heart which constitutes the spiritual blessing, so far forth as the suppliant himself is concerned; and this exercise is never produced, only in so far as it is preceded by dependent and anxious desire for the blessing sought. When the supplication is for spiritual blessing upon another individual, two minds are blessed by the answer—the individual prayed for, and the individual who prays. And if a thousand individuals desired spiritual mercies for that soul, God would be glorified by a thousand hearts, and a thousand hearts would be reciprocally blessed by the answer.

The time may come when all the angels in heaven and all the saints upon earth will be blessed by mercy bestowed upon a single individual. When the last unregenerated sinner stands in solitary and awful rebellion upon the earth, should tidings be circulated through earth and heaven that he had submitted himself to God, and that his affections began to take hold on Christ, every being in the universe who had strongly desired the conversion of the last sinner would feel the thrill of "glory to God and good-will to men" arise in his soul. It follows, therefore, that a fervent, importunate state of mind is, from the nature of the case, necessary, in order that God may be glorified and man blessed by the duty of prayer. It was in view of these constitutional principles that Jesus constantly taught the necessity of desire and importunity, in order that mercies might be received in answer to the supplication of saints.*

The Importance of Faith and a Spirit of Dependence upon God as Concomitants of Acceptable Prayer.

The necessity of faith, as a primary element in all acceptable religious exercises, has already been noticed. A feeling of entire dependence upon God for spiritual mercies is the only right feeling, because it is the only true feeling. As a matter of fact, the soul is entirely dependent upon God for spiritual mercies; truth, therefore, requires that our dependence should be acknowledged and felt.

* Matt. v, 6; Luke xi, 5–10, and xviii, 1–14.

But, further, without faith in God as the immediate bestower of mercies in answer to prayer, he could not be honored for blessings received. Suppose two individuals desired with equally strong feelings the same blessing, and that both received it: each would rejoice alike in its reception. But suppose there was this difference in their state of mind: one regarded the blessing as coming immediately from God in answer to prayer, the other did not. The result would be, that the one who had faith in God would be filled with love to his Maker for the mercy, the other would rejoice in himself; or, at least, he would not rejoice in God. In the one case, God would be honored and praised for his acts of grace; in the other, he would neither be honored nor loved for his goodness. We do not present this illustration as applicable in all its bearings, because we do not suppose that the unregenerate ever truly desire spiritual blessing till they are convicted of sin; but it will make the point clear to the reason of every one, that God can not be honored without faith; and, therefore, "without faith it is impossible to please him."

It is necessary, according to the foregoing view of the subject, in order to offer acceptable prayer, that men should possess a spirit of faith and dependence upon Christ. The principle upon which Christ acted in relation to this subject, as well as his instruction concerning the duty of prayer, fully confirm the preceding thoughts. He seldom performed an act of mercy, by miracle or otherwise, unless those who received the mercy could see the hand of God in the blessing. "If thou canst believe, thou mayest be cleansed," was his habitual sentiment; as if he had said, Your desire for the blessing is manifest by your urgent requests; now, if you can have faith to see God in the blessing, so that he will be honored and praised for conferring it, I will grant it; but if you have no faith, you can receive no favor.

And, again, in order that the believer might be brought into a state of dependence, and have his faith quickened every time that he presented his supplications to God, Jesus said, looking forward to the time when he would have perfected his ministry and atonement, "Hereafter ye shall ask me nothing; but whatsoever ye ask the Father in my name," that is, depending on me, the atoning, interceding Savior, "he will do it." And in another place he promised, "Whatsoever ye ask the Father in my name I will do it." Thus does the instruction of the Savior make the believer entirely dependent upon himself when he approaches the mercy-seat of the Most High. As the Jews were constantly to call to mind the deliverance from Egypt, in order that their feelings might be moved to love, dependence, and faith towards their temporal Deliverer, so Christians are to call to mind the deliverance from spiritual bondage by the sacrifice of Christ, in order that they may realize their dependence, and be inspired with a spirit of faith and love towards their spiritual Deliverer. And because believers can thus depend upon Christ, and feel the mercy of God as it is manifested in the atonement, they are constituted "priests to offer up spiritual sacrifices, acceptable to God through Jesus Christ."

II.—Praise.

The truth which has been demonstrated in previous chapters is again assumed, that the manifestations of God in Christ Jesus would, when brought into efficient contact with the soul, produce that active holiness in the heart which is man's greatest good. And as the end to be accomplished depends, under God, on those truths which are developed in the great plan of mercy being impressed upon the mind and the heart, it follows that those means would be used which, from their nature, are best adapted to give influence and impressiveness to the great truths of Revelation.

The influence of music upon the emotions of the soul is well known to every one:

"There is in souls a sympathy with sounds."

The soul is awakened, and invited by the spirit of the melody to receive the sentiment uttered in the song. Sweet, affecting music—not the tone of the piano, nor the peals of the organ, but a melodious air, sung by strong and well-disciplined voices, and accompanied by the flute and viol—such music reaches the fountains of thought and feeling, and,

"Untwisting all the links that tie
The hidden soul of harmony,"

it tinges the emotions with its own hues, whether plaintive or joyous; and it fosters in the heart the sentiment which it conveys, whether it be love of country or of God, admiration of noble achievement or of devoted and self-sacrificing affection.

The power of music to fix in the memory the sentiment with which it is connected, and to foster it in the heart, has been understood in all ages of the world. Some of the early legislators wrote their laws in verse, and sung them in public places. And many of the earliest sketches of primitive history are in the measures of lyric poetry. In this manner the memory was aided in retaining the facts; the ear was invited to attend to them; imagination threw around them the drapery of beauty, dignity, or power; and then music conveyed the sentiment, and mingled it with the emotions of the soul. It was in view of the power of music, when united with sentiment adapted to affect the heart, that one has said, "Permit me to write the ballads of a nation, and I care not who makes her laws."

When the effects of music and poetry upon the soul are considered, we can perceive their importance as a means of fostering the Christian virtues in the soul of the believer. They should be used to convey to the mind sublime and elevating conceptions of the attributes of Jehovah—to impress the memory with the most affecting truths of revelation; and especially to cherish in the heart tender and vivid emotions of love to Christ, in view of the manifestations of divine justice and mercy exhibited in his ministry, his passion, and his sacrifice.*

There can not be found, in all the resources of thought, material which would furnish sentiment for music so subduing and overpowering as the history of Redemption. There is the life of Jesus, a series of acts, godlike in their benevolence; connected at times with exhibitions of divine power and of human character in their most affecting aspects. And as the scenes of Christ's eventful ministry converge to the catastrophe, there is the tenderness of his love for the disciples; the last supper; the scene in Gethsemane; the Mediator in the Hall of Judgment, exhibiting the dignity of truth and conscious virtue, amidst the tempest of human passion by which he is surrounded. Then the awful moral and elemental grandeur of the crucifixion—the Savior, nailed to the cross by his own creatures, crying, "Father, forgive them, for they know not what they do;" and then, while darkness shrouds the sun, and "nature through all her works gives signs of woe," he cries, "It is finished! and gave up the ghost." Thus did the dark stream of human depravity roll,

> "Till a rainbow broke upon its gloom,
> Which spanned the portals of the Savior's tomb."

Such exhibitions of sublimity and power, when clothed with the influence of music, and impressed

---

* "The proper drapery for music is truth. It is its only apparel, whether as applied to God, or as used for the cultivation of man."—*Erasmus.*

upon a heart rendered sensitive by divine influence, are adapted to make the most abiding and blessed impressions:

"My heart, awake!—to feel is to be fired;
And to believe, Lorenzo, is to feel."

It follows, from the preceding views, that in selecting the means to impress the mind with religious truth and the heart with pious sentiment, music and poetry could not be neglected. There is not in nature another means which would compensate for the loss of their influence. We do not mean to say that their influence is as great as some other means in impressing the truths of Revelation upon the soul; but their influence is peculiar and delightful, and without it the system of means would not be perfect.

We see, therefore, the reasons why music and poetry were introduced as a means of impressing revealed truth, both under the old and the new dispensations. Moses not only made the laws, but he made, likewise, the songs of the nation; these songs, in some instances, all the people were required to learn, in order that their memory might retain, and their heart feel, the influence of the events recorded in their national anthems.

Music held a conspicuous place in the worship of the Temple; and under the new dispensation it is sanctioned by the express example of Jesus, and specifically commanded by the apostles. The example is given in connection with the institution of the eucharist, which was to commemorate the most affecting scene in the history of God's love; and the command is in such words as indicate the effects of music upon the heart: "Speaking to yourselves in psalms, and hymns, and spiritual songs, singing, and making melody in your heart to the Lord; giving thanks always, for all things, unto God and the Father, in the name of our Lord Jesus Christ." Upon this subject, as upon some others, the apostolic Churches fell into some abuses; yet the high praises of God and the Lamb have always been celebrated in poetry and music by the Church of Christ. One of the first notices of the Christians by pagan writers speaks of them as "singing a hymn to Christ, as to a god;" thus showing that the principles established in the preceding views were recognized by the early disciples, who used music as a means of fostering in their hearts love to the Savior.

As in the case of the primitive Christians, so every regenerated heart delights in such spiritual songs as speak of Christ as an atoning Savior. And those only are qualified to write hymns for the Church whose hearts are affected by the love of Jesus. On this account some of the hymns of Cowper, Charles Wesley, Watts, and Newton, will last while the Church on earth lasts, *and perhaps longer.* Thousands of Christian hearts have glowed with emotion, while they sung—

"There is a fountain filled with blood,
 Drawn from Immanuel's veins;

PLAN OF SALVATION. 215

Or,
> And sinners plunged beneath that flood
> Lose all their guilty stains."

> "Rock of Ages, cleft for me,
> Let me hide myself in thee."

Thousands have been awakened to duty and to prayer by that solemn hymn—

> "Lo, on a narrow neck of land,
> 'Twixt two unbounded seas I stand,
> Secure, insensible!"

And it would not have been possible for any but a Christian poet to have written the lines—

> "Her noblest life my spirit draws
> From his dear wounds and bleeding side."

III.—PREACHING.

It has been said that the truths and manifestations of Revelation are the elements of moral power, which, being brought into efficient contact with the soul, are effective in rectifying and regulating its exercises. A medicine may be prepared in which are inherent qualities adapted to remove a particular disease; but in order to the accomplishment of its appropriate effect it must be brought to act upon the body of the patient. And if the disease has rendered the patient not only unconscious of his danger, but has induced upon him a deep lethargy of mind, it would be necessary that the physician should arouse his dormant faculties in order that he might receive the medicine which would restore him to health. So with the moral diseases of the soul: the attention and sensibilities of men must be awakened, in order that the truth may affect their understanding, their conscience, and their heart. Whatever, therefore, is adapted to attract the attention and move the sensibilities, at the same time that it conveys truth to the mind, would be a means peculiarly efficient to impress the Gospel upon the soul.

There are but two avenues through which moral truth reaches the soul; and there are but two methods by which it can be conveyed through those avenues. By the living voice, truth is communicated through the ear; and by the signs of language it is communicated through the eye. The first of these methods, the living voice, has many advantages over all other means in conveying and impressing truth. It is necessary that an individual should read with ease in order to be benefited by what he reads. The efforts which a bad reader has to make, both disincline him to the task of reading and hinder his appreciation of truth. Besides, a large proportion of the human family can not read, but all can understand their own language when spoken. In order, therefore, that the whole human family might be instructed, the living speaker would be the first and best, and the natural method.

The living speaker has power to arrest attention, to adapt his language and illustrations to the character and occupation of his audience, and to accompany his communications with those emotions and gestures which are adapted to arouse and impress his hearers.

It is evident from these considerations that among the means which God would appoint to disseminate his truth through the world, the living teacher would hold a first and important place. This result is in conformity with the arrangements of Jesus. He appointed a living ministry, endowed them with the ability to speak the languages of other nations, and commissioned them to go into all the world and preach the Gospel to every creature.

In connection with this subject there is one other inquiry of importance. It concerns not only the harmony of the Gospel system with the nature of things, but likewise the harmony of apostolic practice with what has been shown to be necessary in order that the truths of the Gospel might produce their legitimate effect upon the mind.

It has been demonstrated that a sense of man's guilt and danger must exist in the mind before there can be gratitude and love to the being who removes the guilt and rescues from the danger. It has likewise been noticed, as a self-evident principle, that before repentance there must be conviction of sin. A sense of guilt and error must necessarily precede reformation of life. A man can not conscientiously turn from a course of life and repent of past conduct unless he sees and feels the error and the evil of that course from which he turns. To suppose that a man would turn from a course of life which he neither thought nor felt to be wrong or dangerous is to suppose an absurdity. It follows, therefore, that the preacher's first duty in endeavoring to reclaim men to holiness and to God would be, in all cases, to present such truths as are adapted to convict their hearers of their spiritual guilt and danger. As God has constituted the mind, repentance from sin and attainment to holiness would forever be impossible on any other conditions.

But the same truths would not convict all men of sin. In order to convict any particular man, or class of men, of sin, those facts must be fastened upon with which they have associated the idea of moral good and evil, and concerning which they are particularly guilty. Thus, in the days of the apostles the Gentiles could not be convicted of sin for rejecting and crucifying Christ; but, it being a fact in the case of the Jews that all their ideas of good and evil, both temporal and spiritual, were associated with the Messiah, nothing in all the catalogue of guilt would be adapted to convict them of sin so powerfully as the thought that they had despised and crucified the Messiah of God.

On the other hand, the heathen, upon whom the charge of rejecting Christ would have no influence, could be convicted of sin only by showing them the falsehood and folly of their idolatry, the holy character of the true God, and the righteous and spiritual nature of the law which they were bound to obey, and by which they would finally be judged. The first preachers of the Gospel, therefore, in conformity with these principles, would aim first, and directly, to convince their hearers of their sins, and in accomplishing this end they would fasten upon those facts in which the guilt of their hearers more particularly consisted. And then, when men were thus convicted of their guilt, the salvation through Christ from sin and its penalty would be pressed upon their anxious souls; and they would be taught to exercise faith in Jesus as the meritorious cause of life, pardon, and happiness.

Now, the apostolical histories fully confirm the fact that this course—the only one consistent with truth, philosophy, and the nature of man—was the course pursued by the primitive preachers.

The first movement after they were endowed with the gift of tongues and filled with the Holy Ghost, was the sermon by Peter on the day of Pentecost, in which he directly charged the Jews with the murder of the Messiah, and produced in thousands of minds conviction of the most pungent and overwhelming description. At Athens, Paul, in preaching to the Gentiles, pursued a different course. He exposed the folly of their idolatry, by appealing to their reason and their own acknowledged authorities. He spoke to them of the guilt which they would incur if they refused, under the light of the Gospel, to forsake the errors, which God, on account of past ignorance, had overlooked. He then closed by turning their attention to the righteous retributions of the eternal world, and to the appointed day when men would be judged by Jesus Christ according to his Gospel.

The manner in which the apostles presented Christ

crucified to the penitent and convicted sinner, as the object of faith and the means of pardon and the hope of glory, is abundantly exhibited in the Acts of the Apostles, and in their several epistles to the Churches.

Thus did God, by the appointment of the living preacher as a means of spreading the Gospel, adapt himself to the constitution of his creatures; and the apostles, moved by divine guidance, likewise adapted the truth which they preached to the peculiar necessities and circumstances of men.

Chapter XVIII.

CONCERNING THE AGENCY OF GOD IN CARRYING ON THE WORK OF REDEMPTION, AND THE MANNER IN WHICH THAT AGENCY IS EXERTED.

God having thus devised the plan, and manifested the truth, and instituted the means of redemption, the inquiry naturally presents itself: In what way would he put the plan into operation, and give efficiency to the means of grace?

We can not suppose that God would put his own institution beyond his power, or that he would leave it to be managed by the imperfect wisdom, and the limited power of human instruments. God would not prepare the material, devise the plan, adapt the parts to each other, furnish the instruments for building, and then neglect to supervise and complete the structure. God has put none of his works beyond his power; and especially, in a plan of which he is the author and architect, reason suggests that he would guide it to its accomplishment. The inquiry is: By what agency, and in what way, would the power of God be exerted, in carrying into efficient operation upon the souls of men the system of saving mercy?

In relation to the character of the agency, the solution is clear. The agency by which the Plan of

Salvation would be carried forward to its ultimate consummation would be spiritual in its nature; because God is a spirit, and the soul of man is a spirit, and the end to be accomplished is to lead men to worship God " in spirit and in truth."

In relation to the mode of the Spirit's operation, some things belong to that class of inquiries upon which the mind may exert its powers in vain. The mode by which God communicates life to any thing in the vegetable, animal, or spiritual world, lies beyond the reach of the human intellect. But although man can not understand the *modus operandi* of the divine mind in communicating life, yet the manifestations of life and the medium through which it operates are subjects open to human examination. Whether the influence of the Spirit be directly upon the soul, or mediately by means of truth, the end accomplished would be the same. The soul might be quickened to see and feel the power of the truth; or, by the Spirit, truth might be rendered powerful to affect the soul. The wax might be softened to receive the impression, or the seal heated, or a power exerted upon it, to make the impression on the wax; or both might be done, and still the result would be the same. It is not only necessary that the metal should be prepared to receive the impression of a die, but it is likewise necessary that the die should be prepared and adapted to the particular kind of metal, the image and superscription of the king put upon it, the machinery prepared and adapted to hold the die and apply it to the metal; and after all these necessary things are done, the coin can never be made unless power is exerted to strike the die into the metal, or the metal into the die. So it is in the processes of the spiritual world: the material (*mankind*) must be prepared; the die (*the truth of the Gospel system*) must be revealed and adapted to the material; and the image to be impressed upon human nature (*the Lord Jesus Christ*) and the superscription (*glory to God and good-will to men*) must be cut upon the die; then the *means* of bringing the truth into contact with the material must be provided; and after all these preparations and adaptations, there must be the power of the Holy Spirit to guide the whole process, and to form the image of Christ in the soul.

The foregoing is a complicated analogy, but not more complicated than are the processes of the animal and spiritual world. Look at the human body, with its thousands of adaptations, all of them necessary to the system, the whole dependent upon the use of means for the supply of animal life; and yet deriving from God its rational life, which operates through and actuates the whole. In like manner the Spirit of God operates through and guides the processes of the Plan of Salvation.

The Scriptures reveal the truth clearly, that the Spirit of God gives efficiency to the means of grace. And not only this, but he operates in accordance with those necessary principles which have been developed in the progress of these chapters. Christ instructed his disciples to expect that he would send the Holy Spirit; and when he is come, said Jesus, " He will reprove the world of sin, of righteousness, and of judgment;" that is, the Holy Spirit will produce conviction of sin in the hearts of the unsanctified and impenitent—the office-work of the Spirit of God in relation to the world is to convince of sin. In relation to the saints he exercises a different office. He is their Comforter. He takes of the things that belong to Jesus and shows them to his people;* that is, he causes the people of God to see more and more of the excellency and the glory and the mercy manifested in a crucified Savior; and by this blessed influence they " grow in grace and in the knowledge of Jesus Christ." Christ, by his ministry and death, furnished the facts necessary for human salvation; the Holy Spirit uses those facts to convict and sanctify the heart. Paul, in a passage already noticed, alludes to the influence of the Spirit operating by the appointed means of prayer or devout meditation: " But we all, with open face, beholding as in a glass the glory of the Lord, are changed into the same image, from glory to glory, *even as by the Spirit of the Lord.*"

Further: At what juncture in the progress of the great Plan of Salvation would this agency be most powerfully exerted? We answer, at the time when the whole moral machinery of the dispensation, through which the effect was to be produced, was completed. Whatever is designed and adapted to produce a

---

* John xvi, 7–14.

definite result as an instrument must be completed before it is put into operation, otherwise it will not produce the definite effect required. An imperfect system put into operation would produce an imperfect result. Here a special effect was to be produced; it was necessary, therefore, that the truth should be revealed and the manifestations all made before the power was imparted to give them effect.

Under the new dispensation the greatest and most imposing manifestations were the death, resurrection, and ascension of Jesus. Had the system been put into operation before these crowning manifestations were made, the great end of the Gospel would not have been accomplished. It follows, then, that the material would be first prepared, the manifestations made and adapted to the material, the appropriate means ordained, and then the agency of the Spirit would be introduced to guide the dispensation to its ultimate triumphs, and to give efficiency to its operations.

These deductions harmonize with the teachings of the Scriptures:

First. They expressly teach, that without the agency of God, no perfect result is accomplished.

Second. They everywhere represent that the divine agency is exerted through the truth upon the soul, or exerted to awaken the soul to apprehend and receive the truth.

Third. The Spirit was not fully communicated until the whole economy of the Gospel Dispensation was completed. The apostles were instructed to assemble at Jerusalem after the ascension, and wait till they were endued with power from on high. On the day of Pentecost the promised Spirit descended. The apostles at once perceived the spiritual nature of Christ's kingdom. They spoke in demonstration of the Spirit, and with power. Men were convicted of sin in their hearts; sinners were converted to Christ by repentance and faith; and under the guidance of that Divine Spirit the Plan of Salvation moves on to its high and glorious consummation, when the "kingdoms of this world shall become the kingdoms of our Lord and his Christ." "Amen: even so, come Lord Jesus!"

Chapter XIX.

CONCERNING THE PRACTICAL EFFECTS OF THE SYSTEM.

The evidence which the Lord Jesus Christ proposed as proof of the divinity of the Gospel system was its practical effect upon individuals who receive and obey the truth. "If ye do of the works, ye shall know of the doctrine, whether it be of God." If a sick man calls a physician, who prescribes a certain medicine, which, by his receiving it according to the directions, cures him, he then knows both the efficacy of the medicine and the skill of the physician. Experience is evidence to the saints of the divinity of the system. And its effect in restoring the soul to moral health is evidence to the world of the divine efficacy and power of its doctrines. "By their fruits ye shall know them." In closing our volume, therefore, we have now only briefly to inquire: What are the ascertained practical effects of faith in Christ?

We shall not refer to the moral condition of man in countries under the influence of the Gospel, compared with his condition in pagan lands. We will not dwell upon the fact which, of itself, is sufficient to establish at once and forever the divine origin of evangelical religion and the truth of the distinctive views developed in the preceding chapters—that the most holy men and women that have ever lived have been those who exercised most constant and implicit faith in Christ. Passing these facts, important in themselves, we will close our volume by a statement of facts concerning the present influence of faith in Christ upon individuals now living, and subject to the examination of any one who might be skeptical upon the subject.

The following is a true statement of the influence of the religion of Jesus upon several individual members of a village Church in one of the United States. It is composed of members of common intelligence, and those in the common walks of life. Other Churches might have been selected, in which, perhaps, a greater number of interesting cases might have been found; and there are other individuals in this Church that would furnish as good an illustration of the power of the Gospel as some of those which are noticed below. This Church has been selected because the writer had a better opportunity of visiting it, in order to obtain the facts, than any other in which he knew the power of the religion of Christ was experienced.

With the individuals spoken of I am well acquainted, having frequently conversed with them all on the subjects of which I shall speak. Their words in all cases may not have been remembered, but the sense is truly given.

CASE 1.—An old man who has been a professor

of religion from early life. He was once a deacon or elder of the Church. Twenty years ago he was struck with paralysis, by which he has been ever since confined almost entirely to his room. His situation is one that, to a mind which had no inward consolation, would be irksome in the extreme. His books are the Bible and one or two volumes of the old divines. He is patient and happy; and speaking of the love of Christ almost invariably suffuses his eyes with tears. He delights to dwell on religious subjects; and to talk with a pious friend of the topics which his heart loves gives him evident delight. Recently his aged companion, who had trodden the path of life with him from youth to old age, died in his presence. She died what is called by Christians a triumphant death. Her last words were addressed to her children who stood around: "I see the cross." A gleam of pleasure passed over her features, her eyes lighted up with peculiar brightness; she said, "Blessed Jesus, the last hour is come; I am ready!" and thus she departed. At her death the old man wept freely and wept aloud; but his sorrow, he said, was mingled with a sweet joy. How desolate would have been the condition of this poor cripple for the last twenty years without the consolations of faith in Christ! And when his aged companion died, who had for years sat by his side, how appalling would have been the gloom that would have settled upon his soul, had not his mind been sustained by heavenly hope! His case shows that the religion of Christ will keep the affections warm and tender even to the latest periods of old age, and give happiness to the soul under circumstances of the most severe temporal bereavement.

CASE 2.—*A converted atheist.* I knew that there were those in the world who professed to doubt the existence of a God; but I had met with no one in all my intercourse with mankind who seemed so sincerely and so entirely an atheist as the individual whose case is now introduced. The first time that I met him was at the house of his son-in-law, a gentleman of piety and intelligence. His appearance was that of a decrepit, disconsolate old man. In the course of conversation he unhesitatingly expressed his unbelief of the existence of a God, and his suspicion of the motives of most of those who professed religion. I learned from others that he had ceased in some measure to have intercourse with men; had become misanthropic in his feelings, regarding mankind in the light of a family of sharks preying upon each other; and his own duty, in such a state of things, he supposed to be to make all *honest* endeavors to wrest from the grasp of others as much as he could. He used profane language, opposed the temperance reformation, and looked with the deepest hatred upon the ministers of religion. His social affections seemed to be withered, and his body, sympathizing, was distorted and diseased by rheumatic pains.

1. This old man had for years been the subject of special prayer on the part of his pious daughter and his son-in-law; and he was finally persuaded by them

to attend a season of religious worship in the Church of which they were members. During these services, which lasted several days, he passed from a state of atheism to a state of faith. The change seemed to surprise every one, and himself as much as any other. From being an atheist, he became the most simple and implicit believer. He seemed like a being who had waked up in another world, the sensations of which were all new to him; and although a man of sound sense in business affairs, when he began to express his religious ideas his language seemed strange and incongruous, from the fact that, while his soul was now filled with new thoughts and feelings, he had no knowledge of the language by which such thoughts are usually expressed. The effects produced by his conversion were as follows, stated at one time to myself, and upon another occasion to one of the most eminent medical practitioners in this country: One of the first things which he did after his conversion was to love, in a practical manner, his worst enemy. There was one man in the village who had, as he supposed dealt treacherously with him in some money transactions which had occurred between them. On this account, personal enmity had long existed between the two individuals. When converted, he sought his old enemy, asked his forgiveness, and endeavored to benefit him by bringing him under the influence of the Gospel.

2. His benevolent feelings were awakened and expanded. His first benevolent offering was twenty-five cents, in a collection for charitable uses. He now

gives very liberally, in proportion to his means, to all objects which he thinks will advance the interest of the Gospel of Christ. Besides supporting his own Church and her benevolent institutions, no enterprise of any denomination which he really believes will do good fails to receive something from him, if he has the means. During the last year he has given more with the design of benefiting his fellow-men than he had done in his whole life-time before.

3. His affections have received new life. He said to me, in conversation upon the subject: "One part of the Scriptures I feel to be true—that which says, 'I will take away the stony heart out of your flesh, and I will give you a heart of flesh.' Once I seemed to have no feeling; now, thank God, I can feel. I have buried two wives and six children, but I never shed a tear—I felt hard and unhappy—now my tears flow at the recollection of these things." The tears at that time wet the old man's cheeks. It is not probable that, since his conversion, there has been a single week that he has not shed tears; before conversion he had not wept since the age of manhood. An exhibition of the love of Christ will, at any time, move his feelings with gratitude and love, until the tears moisten his eyes.

4. Effect upon his life. Since his conversion he has not ceased to do good as he has had opportunity. Several individuals have been led to repent and believe in Christ through his instrumentality. Some of these were individuals whose former habits ren-

dered a change of character very improbable in the eyes of most individuals. (One of them, who had fallen into the habit of intemperance, is now a respectable and happy father of a respectable Christian family.) He has been known to go to several families on the same day, pray with them, and invite them to attend religious worship on the Sabbath. And when some difficulty was stated as a hindrance to their attendance, he has assisted them to buy shoes, and granted other little aids of the kind, in order that they might be induced to attend divine service.*

5. Effect upon his happiness. In a social meeting of the Church where he worships I heard him make

---

* Since the first edition of this volume was issued, a most remarkable fact concerning this old man has come to the knowledge of the author. When converted one of his first acts, although he had heard nothing of any such act in others, was to make out a list of all his old associates then living within reach of his influence. For the conversion of these he determined to labor as he had opportunity, and pray daily. On his list were one hundred and sixteen names, among whom were skeptics, drunkards, and other individuals as little likely to be reached by Christian influence as any other men in the region. Within two years from the period of the old man's conversion one hundred of these individuals had made a profession of religion. We can hardly suppose that the old man was instrumental in the conversion of all these persons; yet the fact is one of the most remarkable that has been developed in the progress of Christianity.

such an expression as this: "I have rejoiced but once since I trusted in Christ—that has been all the time." His state of mind may be best described in his own characteristic language. One day he was repairing his fence. An individual passing addressed him: "Mr. ——, you are at work all alone." "Not alone," said the old man, "God is with me." He said that his work seemed easy to him, and his peace of mind continued with scarcely an interruption. I saw him at a time when he had just received intelligence that a son, who had gone to the South, had been shot in a personal altercation in one of the Southern cities. The old man's parental feelings were moved; but he seemed, even under this sudden and most distressing affliction, to derive strong consolation from trust in God.

6. Physical effects of the moral change. As soon as his moral nature had undergone a change, his body, by sympathy felt the benign influence. His countenance assumed a milder and more intelligent aspect. He became more tidy in his apparel, and his "thousand pains," in a good measure, left him. In his case, there seemed to be a renovation both of soul and body.

This case is not exaggerated. The old man is living, and there are a thousand living witnesses to this testimony, among whom is an intelligent physician, who learned the old man's history of his feelings; and having known him personally for years, the obvious effects which the faith in Christ had produced in this case, combined with other influences by which he was surrounded, led him seriously to examine the subject of religion as it concerned his own spiritual interest. By this examination he was led to relinquish the system of "rational religion," as the Socinian system is most inappropriately called by its adherents, and profess his faith in orthodox religion.

CASE 3.—Two individuals who have always been poor in this world's goods, but who are rich in faith. Many years ago they lived in a new settlement, where there were no religious services. The neighborhood, at the suggestion of one of its members, met together on the Sabbath, to sing sacred music and to hear a sermon read. Those sermons were the means of the conversion of the mother of the family. She lived an exemplary life; but her husband still continued impenitent, and became somewhat addicted to intemperance. Some of the children of the family, as they reached mature years, were converted; the husband, and finally, after a few years, all the remaining children, embraced religion. From the day of the husband's conversion he drank no more liquor, and, he says, he always, afterwards thought of the habit with abhorrence. The old people live alone. The old woman's sense of hearing has so failed that she hears but imperfectly. When the weather will allow, she attends Church regularly, but sometimes hears but little of the sermon. She sits on the Sabbath, and looks up at the minister, with a countenance glowing with an interested and happy expression. She has joy to know that the minister is preaching about Christ. The minister once described religion possessed, as a spring of living water flowing from the rock by the way-side, which yields to the weary traveler refreshment and delight; the old lady, at the close, remarked, with meekness, "I hope I have drank, many times, of those sweet waters."

Except what concerns their particular domestic duties, the conversation of this aged pair is almost entirely religious. They are devout, and very happy in each other's society. And sometimes, in their family devotions and religious conversations, their hearts glow with love to God. They look forward to death with the consoling hope that they will awake in the likeness of the glorious Savior, and so "be forever with the Lord."

CASE 4.—A female who early in life united with the Church, and conscientiously performed the external duties of Christian life. She had, for many years, little if any happiness in the performance of her religious duties, yet would have been more unhappy if she had not performed them. She married a gentleman who, during the last years of his life, was peculiarly devoted. During this period, in attending upon the means of grace, she experienced an entire change in her religious feelings. She felt, as she says, that "now she gave up all for Christ. She felt averse to every thing which she believed to be contrary to his will. To the will of Jesus she could now submit forever, with joyful and entire confidence. She now loved to pray, and found happiness in obeying the Savior." She made, as she believes, at that time an entire surrender of all her interests, for time and eternity, to Christ, and since then her labors in his service have been happy labors. Before they were constrained by conscience, now they are prompted by the affections. She does not think she was not a Christian before. She had repented in view of the law; but she had not, till the time mentioned, exercised affectionate faith in Christ.* She now often prays most solicitously for the conversion of sinners and the sanctification of the Church. She loves to meet weekly in the female circle for prayer, and labors to induce others to attend with her. Her little son, nine years of age, is, as she hopes, a Christian; and her daughter, just approaching the years of womanhood, has recently united with the Church. Two years since her husband died under circumstances peculiarly afflicting. She prayed for resignation, and never felt any disposition to murmur against the providence of God. She sometimes blamed herself that she had not thought of other expedients to prolong, if possible, the life of one that she loved so tenderly; but to God she looked up with submission, and said in spirit, "The cup that my Father hath mingled for me, shall I not drink it?" Her husband she views as

---

* Are there not many in all the Churches who have been convicted of sin, and who have perhaps repented, but have not exercised full faith in Christ?

a departed saint, whom she expects to meet in a better world. She cherishes his memory with an affection that seems peculiarly sacred; and the remembrance of his piety is a consoling association connected with the recollections of one now in heaven.*

A single incident develops the secret of that piety which gives her peace and makes her useful. One of the last times I saw her she stated, in conversation upon the subject, that a short time before she had read a Sabbath-school book which one of her children had received, in which was a representation of Christ bearing his cross to Calvary. While contemplating this scene, love and gratitude sprang up in her heart, which were subduing, sweet, and peaceful beyond expression! How is it, reader, that the contemplation of such a scene of *suffering* should cause such blessed emotions to spread like a rich fragrance through the soul, and rise in sweet incense to God? It is the holy secret of the cross of Christ, which none but the saints know, and even they can not communicate.†

---

* That the marriage bond becomes more sacred, and the reciprocal duties of affection more tender, between two hearts that both love Jesus, I have no doubt. The feelings of this pious widow favor the supposition, and the facts recorded in the biographies of Edwards Fletcher and Carvosso, fully confirm it.

† Thomas á Kempis endeavored to give expression to the consciousness of the divine life in the soul: "Frequens Christi visitatio cum homine interno, dulcis, sermocinatio, grata consolatio, multa pax," etc.

Supplementary Chapter.

AN OBJECTIVE REVELATION NECESSARY, AS A MEANS OF THE MORAL CULTURE OF MANKIND.

Since the first publication of this volume, the question between those who receive the Christian Scriptures as an authoritative divine revelation, and those who do not, has somewhat varied its form. The discussion for the past few years, both in Europe and America, has been mainly between those who believe in the divine authority of the Christian Revelation as a rule of duty, and those who believe in the authority of Conscience and Reason as the highest guides of man. Neither class altogether rejects the Scriptures; but one receives the Messiah and his teachings as of God; the other receives them as of man.

The arguments by which the inspiration of the sacred Scriptures are usually maintained are well known; and but little can be added to them in their common forms. There is, however, another view which may be taken of the subject—a view which considers a *written* Revelation in the light of the moral wants of man, and as an adapted and necessary means in order to human development. Such a train of thought would correspond with the tenor of the argument in the preceding chapters, and would meet, directly, the position of the transcendental school—that all the moral light which God gives to man is revealed subjectively in the human consciousness, or derived by the unaided reason.

If it can be shown that the moral constitution of man demands a revelation *ab extra*—from without—as its complement, and that the Christian Revelation is the adequate and adapted means by which the moral development of man as a being, and of men as a family, must be secured: if these positions can be established, they will place the Bible upon the basis of moral necessity, because the moral constitution of man implies, in order to its development, a *written Revelation*.

We propose, then, for ourselves and our readers, this inquiry: Is man so constituted by his Creator, that a revelation of *objective truth* (*i. e.*, truth revealed *to* him, not *in* him) is demanded, in order to the right and full development of his moral faculties?

In the first chapters of this volume the fact that man is by nature a religious being is stated and proved; and in succeeding chapters the adaptation of some of the processes by which truth is revealed in the Scriptures is discussed. We propose now to direct our attention to the single inquiry, Whether a *written* Revelation be a demand of man's moral constitution, without which his moral culture is impossible.

There is a FIRST FACT connected with this inquiry which might be assumed; but it will be more satisfactory to exhibit its ground and its relations to our discussion.

Man is a *cultivating* and a *cultivable* being.

Culture improves nature. There is a certain degree of perfection attained, or attainable, by the species of the vegetable and animal kingdoms, which nature of herself produces. Unusual circumstances may produce choice individuals, which are in advance of the natural average; but in succeeding generations, without culture, these will return again to the natural level.

No species of things can improve itself. Culture must in all cases come from man. By his agency individuals of the vegetable and animal kingdoms may be advanced far beyond what is possible for them in their natural state. Most species of fruits are " flat, stale, and unprofitable" by nature, and would always have continued so, unless they had received the aid of human culture. So the domestic animals are molded to beauty and utility only by human culture.

All things below man that have valuable qualities are created capable of culture; but the culture must come, in all cases, from a nature higher than their own. Man is the lord of the lower creation. He advances and improves such species as are profitable for his use, and destroys others. Man is the only cultivator, and for his use and benefit nature is made capable of improvement.

But let us mark especially the correlated fact with which we have especially to do in this discussion.

Man is not only a cultivating, but he is a *cultivable* being. Like the other animal species, there is a certain natural level above which he can not rise without aid from a Being higher than himself. (See chap. i.) This is true of him especially as a *moral being*. In intellectual attainment, and in the *perception* of moral principles, individuals among men have achieved a high position without, as some have supposed, aid from an external revelation. We will concede, if it be desired, that some of the moral precepts of Confucius, Socrates, and Seneca are similar to those of the New Testament. Whatever may be conceded on this point, the fact is historically demonstrated and, as we think, philosophically demonstrated (see "God Revealed in the Process of Creation," etc., Book II), that without aid from above himself, man does not attain to a knowledge of the character of God as his Father, nor to a knowledge of self-denying duty due to all men as his brethren. In this respect man is not an exception to the law that no species can raise itself above its natural condition. The Greeks and Romans had many excellent moral precepts; but in the knowledge of God and of self-denial for the good of men they were never in advance of those whom they designated as barbarians. A knowledge of the true character of God and of benevolent labor for men as brothers is absolutely essential, as we shall see, to human culture and human progress; but all human history and human experience testify that man, unaided, can no more attain to this knowledge than an animal can subdue and discipline itself for domestic uses.

Leaving the preceding observations for the consideration of the reader, we assume again the fact, which will be granted even by those who may doubt in relation to some of the preceding statements, God has created man a *cultivating* and a *cultivable* being, and he is the only being created that possesses the double capability to receive and to impart culture. By his ability as a cultivator, he may elevate others up to the level of his own attainment, and by his capacity for culture the cultivator may himself be cultivated by a superior being. We inquire, then, for the *necessary* and *adapted* means, in order to the full development of man's moral faculties.

We will notice three endowments by which men are particularly distinguished from irrational beings. The union of the three is requisite in producing human development; but the effect of the whole will be perceived more distinctly by first noticing them separately. These distinguishing endowments are *Written Language*, *Faith*, and *Conscience*.

A sign-language is characteristic of man. Although it may not be manifest at the lowest stages of social condition, it is always necessary as the basis of social progress. Beasts make, to a considerable extent, sounds and gestures which are intelligible to each other; but they *can not impress upon matter a perma-*

nent sign of their thought. This is an endowment possessed by humanity alone.

It is not necessary to our argument to discuss the forms of the primitive sign-languages, or whether there were an original language which was the basis of all others.* Whether the process be by one method or another, every settled nation with whose history we are acquainted formed or possessed a sign-language. As nations advance in age, language improves, and the people improve *intellectually* with the language. Colonies carry the parent language into new regions of the world. In the lapse of time, by the intermingling of peoples, old forms and sounds are modified—some words are lost and new ones are admitted; but the attribute of a sign-making and sign-reading being is characteristic of man in all ages, after he leaves the lowest stages of barbarism.

The fact is fairly settled, that without aiding himself by a written language, man can not ascend even to the first stages of civilization. But, when time and settled condition will allow, he makes for himself signs of thought; and although the methods may vary, the result is the same; *the signs written by the*

---

*If the present languages of the world be derived from a common origin (which neither reason nor Scripture requires us to suppose), the various streams must run back to the parent source before the two distinct forms of alphabetic and syllabic writing were originated. The rudimental structure of the alphabetic and syllabic languages are so diverse that they could in no way have been derived the one from the other.

hand of one communicate his thoughts through the eye to the minds of others.

After the language of any people has taken its form, the degree of civilization attained at any time can be ascertained with perfect accuracy by the copiousness of their vocabulary and the shades of discrimination in their definitions. In their written language they accumulate the history, science, and sentiments of the past, and add to these the achievements and experiences of the present. Their words, with fixed definitions, are susceptible of authentication as media of commercial and civil transactions; and, as these are conditions of civilization, nothing can be more apparent than the statement that without a written language civilization is impossible; and if civilization is impossible without a written language, we can not suppose that high moral culture can be attained without an aid which is necessary to the lowest stages of social progress.

As certainly, therefore, as man is constituted to ascend from lower to higher stages of progress, written language is designed as the medium of his social and moral culture; but as neither God nor man, so far as we can see, can use signs in any other way than as objective to the mind itself, hence, if man receives moral culture at all, it must be by fixed signs of thought, presented objectively to the human soul. Signs are the creations of the human mind in which *man embodies his logos;* they are the medium by which the thought of one is conveyed to others; and hence they must be the adapted and only means of moral culture, when man is to act as an instrument in elevating his race.

Written language connects man with the past and the future. In it he must store all he holds valuable or sacred in knowledge. Without it he would be an undeveloped moral being; an infant in knowledge, while old in years and· in crime; a being without science, living mostly in the present, haunted by demons of the imagination, and a prey to human tyrants, as ignorant but more powerful than himself.

But suppose it be granted that without written language man can not receive moral culture; yet are not the signs of that language, and the ideas that they contain, originated by man? And hence while a written language in order to moral culture may be admitted, a revelation of truth other than that originated by man may be denied.

It will be seen, when we come to consider the subject of faith, that, in order that truth may affect the moral character of man and exert upon him an elevating and purifying influence, he must receive it as coming from God, the Lawgiver and Judge of men. But apart from this consideration, which is a vital one in its relation to the subject of moral culture, there are plain evidences which prove that man can not of himself attain to the true idea of the divine character; and hence, if God be ever truly known to men, he must reveal himself in such forms and by such signs as will communicate a true knowledge of his character to the human mind.

We are aware that there are those who believe and teach that the *character* of God, as well as the *being* of a God, is revealed subjectively in men. We will notice the superficial and injurious character of this philosophy in another place; but here we affirm that all history, and the common experience and reason of men, prove the fallacy of such an opinion. A sense, or intuition, or conception (call it what you will) of the existence of a God, is found in all ages, existing in all races of men. It is a universal conviction, and belongs to man as man. But no two men have precisely the same idea of God's *character*. The diversity in one case is as perfect as the unity of the other. Without a revelation men believe that there is a God; but their views of the divine character are as diverse as their languages, and have never risen above the level of heroism, naturalism, and lust, in connection with the natural attributes of wisdom and power. The idea of the existence of God is the idea of being. The idea of character implies quality; to suppose that man has intuitive ideas of either the physical or spiritual qualities of things is absurd.

Again, every man is conscious that he has not himself got an intuitive idea of the character of God. Every man believes that God *is;* but what he is, is with every man matter of reflection, or of faith. The conscious experience of every man is testimony in this case.

It is a fact admitted almost universally, that the

present state of the creation, both moral and physical, is imperfect. Allowing, then (if it be desired), that man has an intuitive idea that a Divine Being, or Beings, exist—how could he get the conception of a perfect character from an imperfect world? If man forms a conception of God's character without revelation, in the present state of things, he must necessarily form a wrong one. Man is imperfect, and nature is imperfect, and therefore there is no archetype from which a true sign of the divine character can be drawn. Hence the histories of man's theologies, in all ages, are histories of errors.

Now, it is a fact which is marked and peculiar that the character of God revealed in the Old Testament is revealed in accordance with the laws by which signs are made to communicate first ideas, and in accordance with the nature of man as a sign-reading being. We have shown in chapters vii and viii that the word Jehovah, signifying merely *divine being— without character*—was clothed with attributes by a process of signs or hieroglyphics which formed the true character of God in the Jewish mind, so far as that character was known under the introductory dispensation. Moses was a sign-maker. His dispensation was one of types.* From the processes and hiero-

---

* Ex. xxv, 40: "Make them after the *pattern* that was showed thee in the mount." See also Acts vii, 44. The Mosaic ceremonies generally are declared to be "patterns [pictures, hieroglyphics] of things in the heavens." (Heb. ix, 23.)

glyphics of his dispensation the ideas of heavenly things were produced. This is expressly affirmed in the New Testament, as it is likewise in the Old.

Under the New Testament Dispensation we have a manifestation of *duty, in the life of Christ, and of love in his* SELF-SACRIFICE, which have given new ideas to the human mind. These are rendered permanent in the written language of the New Testament. In Christ's death " was the love of God manifested"—and man could never have had the idea but by the cross of Christ. *The cross of Christ* is the *sign* of divine love for men. The life of Christ is the sign of human duty. These manifestations are objective to the soul. These ideas, embodied in sign-language, are the material of the highest moral culture. But in order to elevate and purify the soul, *they must become subjective* in the heart, and authoritative with the conscience and the will.

This brings us to the connected subject of *faith*, by which objective Divine Truth becomes subjective in the soul.

Faith, or Credence, like sign-language, distinguishes between man and irrational beings. (The word Credence may be more appropriate as a general term, while we apply the word Faith in a moral sense.) Animals receive knowledge by sensation only; man receives knowledge by sense and by credence. Almost the whole of man's acquired knowledge he obtains by crediting the testimony of others.

In relation to God and the objects of the spiritual

world, faith is *the only* exercise by which we can know them. These are not cognizable by the senses. The being of God may be admitted intuitively, but the character of God can be known only by faith; and *it is the character of God*, NOT THE BEING OF GOD, that is the element of moral culture. In order to the moral effect of the divine character upon the soul, we "must believe not only that *God is*, but that he is a *rewarder of those who diligently seek him.*"

God has so made man that his moral nature is moved and his moral character controlled by faith. If he believes (whether falsely or not) that his neighbor is a bad man, he will feel towards him as if it were so. If he believes with an assured faith certain things in relation to God and duty, he will feel and act as he believes. If a man has faith in truth, he will have a true conscience; but in so far as his faith is false, his conscience will be false; and in relation to duties due to God, if a man has no faith at all, he will have no conscience at all. A man without faith is influenced no more in his character or conduct by the existence and character of God than if there were no God. In the light of such truth, every sound mind ought to see that transcendentalism is a *moral lie.*

God has made the soul of man to recognize him as sovereign, and his will as obligatory. The animal mind reaches up to man, and knows no higher lord. The mind of man by faith reaches up to the Supreme Being, and recognizes duty and obligation to him. Thus man by *faith* and *conscience* becomes responsible as a subject of the divine government, and is thus separated from all inferior things.

Sign-language and *Faith* are correlated in the moral tuition of man. All human progress depends upon faith exercised in testimony, fixed by the settled import of written language. Without credence vocal language might exist, and men might communicate to each other their experiences and observations; but credence alone, in connection with fixed signs of thought, raises man to the contemplation of the past, the future, the spiritual, and the divine.

But all the objects upon which moral culture depends are without the soul. They are not subjective, but objective. Say, if you will, that the idea of a God is an intuition; but what God is has been matter of credence in all time, and with all men. It is unnatural, it is impossible, for man to look into himself for objects of credence. The idea is a preposterous one. Man is created a believing being, and Faith looks out of self for its objects, as naturally as the eye looks out of self to the phenomena of the world of sense.

But in order that the objects of Faith may have subjective efficiency over the affections, the will, and the conscience, man must recognize not only the *rectitude* but the *authority* of the truth presented for credence. This brings us to consider, in connection with Faith, the office of Conscience, without the rectitude and efficiency of which there can be no moral culture.

There are two elements in efficient faith; one

the *form* of the fact, the other the *authority* of the fact. The fact, in order to be efficient within men, must be perceived not only as *truth*, but as *authoritative truth*; that is, perceived as proceeding from a being whose character we love, and whose authority to command we recognize. *The perception of truth does not impart the moral power or the moral disposition to obey the truth.* No man in his senses will say that the man who perceives truth obtains *thereby* a disposition to obey it. Truth has little efficiency for moral culture, unless it be recognized by faith, as grounded in the character and communicated to man by the will of God. Whatever is believed by the soul to be the will of the Divine Lawgiver revealed for man, that conscience will enforce upon the life.

Socrates, Plato, and Seneca uttered much valuable truth, and truth that was *recognized* among the people as coming from the *highest human sources*. But what cared men for the utterances of philosophers? Whose conscience troubles him in our day for not obeying the maxims of the author of Lacon, or the precepts of living or dead moralists? Men are equals; and truth from merely human sources can rise no higher than the *opinions* of equals. It may be, it generally is, believed as truth; but it can have no moral sanction as obligatory upon the life, and therefore can have little influence upon the soul as an element of moral culture.

The greatest difficulty with men is not that they do not perceive truth. Men perceive much moral truth by the force of their own reason; and they assent to much more that is perceived by others. Colton wrote more moral maxims than any man of his age, and violated them all. Instead of the perception of truth being moral culture in his case, it was, as in many other cases, only a light that revealed a deeper debasement. A revelation of truth concerning God and human duty is necessary; but power or disposition to obey the truth is the greater want—*is an absolute necessity*—in order to the moral culture of the soul. A perception of truth without love and obedience is demoralizing. A perception of truth which moves the heart and the will is the process of moral culture.

Both experience and revelation agree in the things which have been said. The teachings of the Messiah himself had no reformatory or sanctifying power, until men believed that they were sanctioned by the Godhead. This Jesus frequently affirmed. The disciples were taught to expect that *when* the resurrection and the advent of the Comforter should have attested the *divinity of his mission*, THEN men would be "convinced of *sin, righteousness,* and *judgment;*" that is, when they saw God in the truth which he taught, they would feel that it was sin to disobey. The words which he had spoken unto them would become spirit and life to their souls, when they were received as the *word of God.*

Now, let us condense and remember the facts which we have considered. The character of Conscience in all religious duties depends upon Faith. Without faith it has no life; with a false faith it is corrupted, and therefore a curse; with a true faith it is living and pure. Conscience in itself is a most potent power, but it is a blind power. It enforces the conduct dictated by a man's faith, *whatever that may be.* But its power for good or evil comes only with a sense of the authority of God. It will enforce no duty nor produce remorse for any neglect of duty, in regard to God, unless faith affirms the act to be sanctioned by the will and authority of God. A sense of right exists in most minds and consciences—so enjoins a right practice towards men—until the mind becomes darkened by a false credence or a wrong practice. But where no faith exists, *conscience never enforces a wrong towards man as a sin against God.* And even in relation to the duties in life which we learn by experience, the conviction of right is often very inefficient; and in relation to the highest social duties, a false credence often makes wrong to be a duty or a privilege.

In relation to God, therefore, and religious duty, faith is the only guide of conscience; and in relation to the practice of right towards men, and more especially the maintenance of right social principles, man is a weak and wandering spirit; and when his conscience dies or is perverted by a false credence or a wrong practice, he has hope of rescue and purity only in a revelation which faith may receive as the will of God, and which conscience will then enforce as duty; the violation of which is sin.*

---

* A fact of importance in this connection it may be profitable to notice—a fact both in revelation and in

From the preceding considerations we might at once deduce a conclusion in favor of an objective revelation, as a necessary requisite in order to human culture. But this conclusion would be a general one, and many who would assent to the general conclusion might not agree that the New Testament is the only perfect and the ultimate revelation of Divine Truth.

Before, therefore, we endeavor to show the adaptedness of the Christian Scriptures as the *only system of Truth*, by which man's moral nature can be rightly

---

human experience. It is not a link in the argument, but it may aid our conviction of the vital importance of the subject. It shows, likewise, the relation of this subject of Divine Culture to the fact stated in an introductory paragraph, that culture of one being must come from another superior to itself. Thus man cultivates nature and God cultivates man.

It is a law of man's nature, that when the truth is perceived in the mind, and its obligation acknowledged, if obedience be not yielded, the conscience grows less potential to enforce the duty. It is a retributive principle incorporated into man's moral constitution, that sin being persisted in against light and obligation, the light becomes darkness in the mind, and the sense of obligation dies in the soul. *This is a natural law.* But a sense of God's special presence reverses this law. The influence of the Holy Spirit awakens again the dying conscience, and illumines again the darkening mind. The evil of sin is again seen and felt. The dead conscience is awakened by the presence of God, and the soul that was sinking under the moral paralysis of sin is offered rescue and called to heaven. Reader, this is your hope—the *miraculous interposition* of the Divine Spirit.

and fully developed, let us notice, in connection, some of the views by which we have argued the necessity of an objective revealment of Divine Truth, in opposition to the false notion that a knowledge of the divine character and of human duty are revealed subjectively in the soul.

Man is created conscious of imperfection and capable of culture.

Man can receive moral culture only by the aid of signs of moral truth embodied in written language.

Man may have by nature an intuition of the being of God, but he has no knowledge of the *character of God;* but that character has been revealed in accordance with the process of linguistic development, and in adaptation to man's nature and wants, in the Old and New Testaments.

Man is a being of Faith, and can be affected by the character and will of God only by the exercise of faith. Faith naturally looks out of self for its objects. The past, the future, God and the spiritual world are without the soul, as revealed by faith.

Man is a being of Conscience; but the character of conscience is determined by faith. Unless faith sees God in truth, conscience will not enforce it on the soul. But it will enforce whatever faith dictates as the character and will of God, whether right or wrong.

Faith is in itself blind. It does not know truth from error; and reason has never had power without revelation to correct its false affirmations. The highest effort of reason is to produce doubt. (See chap. i.) It can not substitute truth for falsehood.

Conscience is blind. It is a potential force, but it follows faith right or wrong; and when faith is false it enforces falsehood in the soul.

Both faith and conscience look to God for authority; and until faith sees God in Truth, Conscience will not convict the soul of guilt for disobedience.

Hence, in the moral culture of the soul, every thing depends on the revealment of truth. But this truth must come to the soul, not as human opinion, or as the utterances of philosophy, but as Truth which Faith and Conscience recognize as rendered obligatory upon man, by the will and authority of God. *Without* revealed Truth, *Reason has no data, Faith is false, and Conscience is corrupt.* The erring nature of man's moral powers, without Revealed Truth, requires a revelation from the Maker. As there can be no moral culture with a false faith and a corrupt or dead conscience, hence a revelation of objective Truth, rendered efficient by the perceived presence and authority of God, *is a moral necessity*, in order to the culture of the human soul.

But in order to the moral culture of man it is not only necessary, as we have seen, that man should receive from a personal God, by faith, a revelation of Truth; but certain characteristics in that truth itself are necessary—characteristics which as we shall now show, mark the New Testament as the inspired, adapted, and final revelation of God to man.

In view, then, of man's character and condition,

notice some characteristics necessary in revealed truth, in order to his perfect and ultimate culture.

A first requisite in the truth itself, in order to moral culture, is, that it should be ultimate and perfect, so that the standard may always be in advance of man's present attainment; and that it should be so revealed as to awaken and encourage aspiration and struggle for conformity to the revealed standard.

Every one will allow that a determination of the soul from evil to good, and a struggle upward, is the only method by which man can possibly attain to a better moral condition.

But in order to awaken interest and promote effort for moral advancement, truth must be so exhibited as to show us our present moral delinquencies and derelictions. This can be done only by presenting precept and example which are above the present moral condition of the soul. It is self-evident that man can not advance to a higher position until he is convinced that his present state is a wrong one, and below attainments which he is under obligation to make. Divine precept and example stand as the embodied model. The effort, by divine aid, for a higher attainment in holy living is the process by which the attainment is secured; and the attainment in which the soul finds its happiness in a spirit of love for Christ and labor of love for man, is the culture that the soul needs; and when divinely illumined by truth, it is the culture which the soul seeks.

Now, do the precepts and examples of the New

Testament furnish authoritative objective truth of this character? Are they such, that while they encourage and aid, they will always be in advance of the soul, leading it up to moral perfection?

About this question there can be no controversy. No man dare deny that if the spirit of the New Testament prevailed on earth, vice and crime and want would cease among men. Neither atheists nor skeptics dare deny that the spirit of the Christian Scriptures is reverent love for God and self-denying, happy love-labor for man. The ultimate good of all men can only be attained by those who possess good of any kind, denying themselves to bring those below them up to the good they enjoy. The New Testament spirit and example is a perfect fulfillment of this requirement. It stands alone, and high as heaven above every thing else known to the human mind in the spirit and practic of self-denying love for the equal temporal and spiritual good of all men. The devil dare not deny that the labor and sacrifice of Christ for the good of men is ultimate. Nothing can be higher, holier, or in any respect better than the precept, the spirit, and the example of the New Testament. It has ever been in advance of human character, and will be till the end of time. It is ultimate in spirit, in precept, and in example; and it is not profane to say that, if there be any other revelation, or if God give any other, it must be a worse one, because there can not be a better.

There is another requisite in the character of revelation necessary to human culture, which we have assumed, but which we will now notice more fully. That requisite is, that the ultimate standard of duty should be given in the form of example.

We need to know not only what we ought to do, but we need to understand the spirit in which a duty should be discharged. A good act may become evil, and have no influence for moral culture, because it is not done in a good spirit. Those who have not the Spirit of Christ are none of his. But an example of forbearance, of firmness, of self-denial, of reproof, of comparison, of forgiveness, of the *manner of conduct* in particular circumstances, is necessary, in order to lead men to understand, and by faith enable them to discharge right duties in a right spirit. (See chap. xvi.)

But example, in order that we may understand the motive and the spirit of duty, is necessary in another particular. General precepts have specific applications; and the best minds are liable to err in the application of general precepts to the varying every-day duties of life. Man is so constituted that perfect knowledge of duty in all specific cases is impossible; he needs, therefore, an ever-present guide, to which he can refer the decision of what is duty in specific cases. There can be no such guide except it be *a model character acting in our circumstances.* The life of Christ is the infallible standard of reference for sinful men acting in a world of sinners. Suppose an absent father should leave his son to manage his affairs during his absence. It would be impossible for him to leave his son specific directions in relation to all cases that might arise in the varied duties of the farm during a long absence. The son, however, has seen the example of his father; he knows perfectly the motives which governed him, and the spirit he manifested. In the application, therefore, of his father's general precepts to specific cases, he involuntarily, naturally, dutifully asks himself, *What would my father do in this case? What would he have me do?* Thus the knowledge of his father's character, life, and spirit, guides him in the application of precept to practice; while at the same time, it reveals the motive and the spirit in which the act should be done.

Other requisites in the character of revealed truth might be added to these; but we will not prolong the chapter. We might show that there should be elements to awaken hope and courage in those who seek the "mark of the prize of the high *culture*," given in the life and spirit of Jesus; and that these elements accompany the precept of the New Testament.

We might show that the question, "What is Truth?" on moral subjects, can never be settled in any individual mind, except by faith and divine authority, and an ultimate example; and that these are given in the written Scriptures.

We might show that there can be no culture of the soul except the motive to action be benevolent; that love of Christ makes God the motive—takes it out of self; and hence acts for Christ's sake are necessarily unselfish acts, and that unselfish action is necessary to moral culture.

We have, we trust, already said enough to aid candid minds to the conclusion that the moral culture of the soul must be accomplished by a system of Truth, revealed objectively in written language, by divine authority; and that the Christian Scriptures contain that system of Truth.

The Scriptures alone possess the characteristics which adapt truth to the ends of moral culture. The believer is made humble by the perfection of Christ's example of love and labor and sacrifice for men—a perfect standard, yet so far in advance of his attainment. Gospel faith, which realizes in the soul that Christ's sacrifice was for him, *will mingle gratitude and love with his humility.* The offer of aid in the moral conflict, of pardon to the penitent, and of divine favor to every one who denies himself and exercises a spirit of affectionate obedience, inspires hope and courage, and gives joy by the way; and, then, Divine Authority, as well as Divine Love, being in the Truth, these govern in harmony the *affections,* the *conscience,* and the *will.*

No man can ever make so high an attainment in moral culture that Christ will not be before him still, as an example and a guide; and yet no man can be so low in moral culture but that the Gospel faith brings to him hope, impulse, direction, and a spiritual benediction; and in whatever stage of progress the Christian may be, whether near the beginning of the race, or so far advanced that temptation has little influence, and habits of holy action are mostly confirmed—at whatever stage of attainment those who lay aside every known sin, and looking to the character of Christ as the goal of moral perfection, run *with what strength they have* for the prize of the high calling of God in Christ Jesus—*all such will receive divine aid and favor by the way.** Progress is the order of the moral as well as the physical world (see "God Revealed in the Process of Creation," etc.), perfection is its end, and the manifestation of God in Christ, revealed in the New Testament, is a necessary element in order to the final consummation.

Leave, then, reader, the transcendental folly of those who would find the perfect character of God revealed subjectively in themselves; or who seek a perfect example in an imperfect humanity. Such a philosophy is shallow and sinful; it is engendered by selfishness, in union with aspiring intellect. Its glare has poison in it; and it dazzles to blind the conceited

---

* The question of perfection, about which good men have often misconceived each other, ought to be considered obsolete. *Men can do what they can do, in the circumstances, and God requires no more.* The call of God is *no more.* The requirement is not ultimated perfection, but progressive perfection. Men are called to aim and strive for the moral perfection set before them in the life of Christ; and he who, like Paul, is a perfect runner toward the goal, is perfect † in in one sense; while not having yet attained the goal, he is imperfect in another.

† This is the plain and undoubted sense of the Scriptures. (See Phil. iii, 7—16.) "Let us, therefore, as many as are perfect, be thus minded."

and superficial thinker. Believe in the Lord Jesus, repent from selfishness, cross your own will, and follow Christ in filial piety to God and love-labor for man, and thou shalt be saved.

CONCLUSION.

ALLOW the author to say, in closing, that it is his opinion, that in view of the reasonings and facts presented in the preceding pages, every individual, who reads the book intelligently, and who is in possession of a sound and unprejudiced reason, will come to the conclusion, that *the religion of the Bible is from God, and divinely adapted to produce the greatest present and eternal spiritual good of the human family.* And if any one should doubt its divine origin (which, in view of its adaptations and its effects as herein developed, would involve the absurdity of doubting whether an intelligent design had an intelligent designer), still, be the origin of the Gospel where it may, in heaven, earth, or hell, the demonstration is conclusive, that it is the only religion possible for man, in order to perfect his nature, and restore his lapsed powers to harmony and holiness.